Praise

'It is time to remove the fog. This book is a simple and practical guide on how to approach and harness data and AI, supported by clever humans, to create better outcomes for your business.'
— **Dr Beatrice Lafon**, ex CEO Claire's, Pimkie, Kondor, Etam Group, T J Hughes, Founder The Business Intelligence Network, Chair/ NED in the Consumer Sector, Founding Member of the Leadership Council at causaLens

'In today's world, harnessing the power of data is not just key to driving successful business strategies, but sustainable ones too. *Data Means Business* provides practical advice and clear frameworks for achieving this, and is a must-read for business leaders looking to harness the power of data to drive positive change.'
— **Adam Elman**, Director of Sustainability – EMEA, Google

'A valuable read for data leaders and learners, providing insightful and pragmatic guidance.'
— **Susie Moan**, Chief Data Officer, Currys Plc

'There is nothing more important in the world of data than using it to drive commercial outcomes – whatever those might be for your organisation. *Data Means Business* is the guide both data and commercial professionals need in order to understand how they can best collaborate and support each other so they can use data for exactly those outcomes. A must-read for all senior leaders!'
 — **Greg Freeman**, CEO, Data Literacy Academy

'Many companies talk about data and AI, but then struggle to deliver. This book gives readers the tools they need to make data and AI a core focus of their growth strategy. A must-read for senior business leaders looking to understand the approach and work required to make this happen.'
 — **Kim Gray**, Non-Executive Director and Executive Coach

'Whilst there are no shortage of "data books" on the market, this one is unashamedly focused on driving commercial outcomes from your business. It sounds obvious, but in this book Jason and Barry manage to stay laser-focused on delivering actual value and using data in practical ways to do so. It is an unpretentious and well-described handbook of tools, examples and questions we should all be using to utilise our data assets to their full potential.'
 — **Barry Panayi**, Partner and Chief Data and Insight Officer, John Lewis Partnership

'In developing our technology strategy that enables our business outcomes, we realised the need to include data. Like technology, articulating the impact of data on business results as an input to drive strategic decisions is difficult to most business leaders. We therefore used business capabilities to translate not just the technology and data capabilities but all key components of our business. Having a common way to describe our organisation has helped facilitate the necessary conversations. These conversations not only educate everyone but help build on the cultural change needed to support a digital journey. This book provides all the stimulus to help facilitate the conversation and make data part of the Business DNA.'

— **Jeroen Akkermans**, Head of Digital Innovation and Enterprise Architecture, DSM-Firmenich

'As the Tech and Data world continues to introduce more jargon, the CDO faces the perpetual challenge of demystifying their value and aligning perspectives from almost everyone in the business on what they should be doing on any given day! *Data Means Business* provides the reassurance and frameworks to help the CDO win by providing practical guidance to focus their efforts on enhancing critical capabilities that matter to the enterprise, unlocking proven approaches to quantify the CDO impact.'

— **Chris Wyard**, Chief Data Officer, Beazley Group

'I loved this book, so much of it resonates with me and is an articulation of my own journey of data discovery over the years. This is not just a book for chief data officers and data management leads as it says in the intro, this is a handbook for any and all CXOs who have responsibility for or an interest in data – and that is *all* of them.'
— **Lorraine Waters**, Chief Data Officer, Global Compliance, HSBC and Top 100 Global Data Power Women 2020

'Intelligent, witty and insightful. Barry and Jason eloquently discuss the challenging nature of business with the complexity of organisational culture to beautifully illustrate a framework to release value and create advantage from data that you may already hold. A must-read for all navigating change and innovation.'
— **Dr Johanna Hutchinson**, Group Chief Data Officer, BAE Systems Plc

'A great guide which I would highly recommend to all Chief Data Officers, future Heads of Data and business leaders to help them on their data journey. Unlike some guides which use technical jargon readily, *Data Means Business* instead offers simple steps to deliver an effective data-led organisation.'
— **Katie Hevey**, Digital and Data Practice Leader, Leathwaite

'Data, like money and people, is an organisation's most precious resource. While finance teams have generations of established practice, the data profession has quickly matured from newborn into an AI-powered infant. As organisations grapple with both data and AI capabilities, only the most adept are seizing the full potential. Jason and Barry's influential book continues to be the North Star for the profession, now modernised for the AI era. Their practical framework is levelling the playing field for leaders who need to build data and AI capability but don't know what excellence looks like. Read this and you will.'

— **Omid Shiraji**, Portfolio CIO, Advisor and Non-executive Director

Second Edition

Data
Means
Business

A practical guide to creating
value from data and AI

Jason Foster and Barry Green

R^ethink

This edition first published in Great Britain in 2025
by Rethink Press (www.rethinkpress.com)

First published in 2021

Contents

Foreword

When Jason and Barry asked me to write the foreword for the first edition of this book, I was flattered, of course, but it took me a while to agree. At first, I wanted to sit them down and point fingers.

'Don't forget to emphasise the importance of data,' I could hear myself preaching. 'Do it again, then keep doing it until you're certain you've got the point across.'

In the end, I needn't have worried. What resulted was a brilliant best-selling text, and both authors deserve huge credit for that.

Then came the request to help with the second edition. Same hesitance, only this time amplified, and not pointed at them. No, dear reader, this time I want to reach out to you. Same concerns, same message and same urgency, but for somewhat different reasons.

Since Jason and Barry decided to set the world straight, we've seen a landslide of innovation. Their original musings were cast in a pre-ChatGPT world, you see. A world where classical information technology (IT) systems reigned and well-trained human professionals worried about the quality of their data and the value it would bring. That was a world of manually hard-coded software and artisan data. Of structured query language (SQL) statements written over days if not weeks, and data strategies crafted like sonnets.

Looking back, it was all rather twee.

Today, things have changed forever. With the arrival of generative artificial intelligence (GenAI), we now see a world where the code itself is just as capable, if not more so than any human able to write it. Born out of rapid innovation in data science, neural networks, vector-based data stores and natural language processing, GenAI models are designed to sample from probability distributions, allowing them to generate a variety of outputs – from natural language to more abstract forms of encoding, like machine language or system commands. They therefore do more than just replicate language, capturing nuanced semantic patterns in their training data, for instance.

Equally important is the configuration of these models – the scale of which has grown to millions or even billions of parameters. This empowers them to effectively encode and 'understand' enormous collections of deeply complex semantic information, by mapping language structures, entities, ideas and relationships. This leads to hitherto unseen capacity to simulate a wide variety of functions that previously required separate representation.

As a result, they aren't merely tools for natural language, but adaptable engines capable of functioning across multiple tasks with heterogeneous requirements – paving the way for more streamlined approaches to systems design. To be concise, they've comfortably assimilated and can skilfully use the combined set of human-centric lexicons and grammars we know as natural language.

Summed up, this amounts to one of two things – either a tremendous opportunity for accelerated innovation and growth, or an existential threat the likes of which we've never seen before. It's not for me to future gaze, so I'll leave it to you to decide.

All that said, there are some obligatory ground rules in place already, and one of those stands out beyond and before all others. So much so that I'll spell it out in a way that can be easily passed on:

There can be no artificial intelligence (AI) without information architecture (IA).

There it is – the first commandment of the AI age, which explains that before any AI model can crawl, let alone run, it must be bootstrapped using well-focused, high-quality data. For all that the world around that data has altered radically, very little has changed regarding how it should be collected, assessed, configured, governed, secured and used. Only its importance has been upgraded.

Where all but recently, data was a back-of-shop concern, barely raising an eyebrow amongst executives, now it's well and truly in the limelight. No longer is it a separate, disparate thing to be pushed and pulled in the shadows. Instead, it's embedded into the very engines that will drive growth from here on. Not only is it your business, but it is *quite literally* your business – the very lifeblood of your enterprise's commerce.

With all that out of the way, hopefully you can understand why I want to sit you down and emphasise the importance of this book. In it, you'll not only find wisdom to keep you profitable and safe, directed and inspired, but refined future-looking necessity. Therefore, I encourage you to read it fully and with care.

In fact, keep this book by your side wherever and whenever possible. Find other books like it and read those too, but all the time, remember that the story has always and will always start with data.

I'll leave the rest to Jason and Barry…

Professor Philip Tetlow PhD, Author, TED Speaker, CEO and CTO

Introduction

In nature everything is interdependent; there are millions of small ecosystems existing together. When they are all connected, they make up our environment. Small changes in one ecosystem can have big impacts on the immediate and overall environment. Plankton disappearing from the sea or honeybee numbers reducing will have effects disproportionate to their overall physical size. These ecosystems are fragile and unexpected change can have catastrophic consequences. It is important to understand and manage our understanding of these interdependencies. By learning and developing our understanding we can continue to enjoy the environment in which we live, even as it evolves.

Darwin's theory of evolution by natural selection provides a way to understand the interdependencies, but also how and why the overall environment has evolved. Evolution is continuous. Business is another example of an ecosystem. Millions of businesses exist in different countries, creating different services and products, seemingly independent of each other. As an ecosystem each business has a set of components, living (people) and non-living (systems), and while it exists for a specific purpose, the dependencies on the overall environment are there.

It is our responsibility as leaders to drive change and manage business not just for profit but for all stakeholders – employees, customers, shareholders, society and the environment. Like the environment, the business ecosystem is changing at a rapid pace. Power in society and the way consumers engage with brands is shifting. Our choice for services has continued to explode. Big technology players are gobbling up market demand and killing off long-established brands. Like evolution, change is continuous.

If we try to manage this change by focusing on only one aspect of the business ecosystem, we are bound to fail. The COVID-19 pandemic highlighted the fragilities of industries, economies and governments, and showed that we are connected, perhaps more than we realised. The ability to adapt in a world where we needed to 'lock down' cities, regions and countries without destroying the social and economic fabric meant that digital enablement was key to protecting our businesses and the broader environment. A digital environment is becoming critical for us to maintain business ecosystems. It is also a natural evolution. An unforeseen virus forced us to innovate and evolve.

We wrote the first edition of this book during the first year of the pandemic. So much has happened since then. In some ways everything has changed (who remembers the 'new normal'?), and in many other ways it's stayed the same. Some of the pre-pandemic world has returned, some of the good things that came from the lockdowns remain, some have gone away for ever.

Remote work, once a necessity, has become a permanent fixture in many industries, reshaping the way we think about office spaces and work-life balance. Digital acceleration driven by the pandemic has continued unabated, with advancements in artificial intelligence (AI), blockchain and the Internet of Things enabling innovation across sectors. Ecommerce has solidified its dominance, the gig economy and fractional careers have expanded, offering both opportunities and challenges for workers worldwide.

Yet not everything changed in the way we might have expected. While the initial surge in community spirit and mutual aid during the pandemic was heartening, some of that momentum waned as societies returned to pre-pandemic routines. The anticipated shift towards more sustainable living practices has been uneven, with significant progress in some areas but persistent challenges in others. The worldwide supply chain disruptions that began during the pandemic have had lasting effects, reminding us of the interconnectedness and fragility of our international economy, the global ecosystem.

What all this has taught us is that as leaders, we need to do things differently to bring about change. We cannot keep doing the same things in the same ways and expecting different results. If we digitise the way we operate, implement faster and connect things in an ethical and responsible way, we can be better prepared for systemic changes to our environment and adapt around what is thrust on us.

But being digital is not as simple as implementing technology. We need to think about re-imaging processes and how people interact and engage. That leaves one major component missing, which dooms digital to fail if it's not mastered.

Data – electronic information stored in systems – is a key component that needs to be better connected, understood, managed and used for the evolution of business. To build a new ecosystem we need to digitise the inputs. Key dependencies to this are process, people and culture. Process gives data context. People interact with processes to create data. Data, people and process are influenced by the culture in which data is created. Really, we need to look at data as a social science – not only through a digital lens, but as a conduit to change. Technology will be needed to ensure we reuse, maintain and manage data. But this should not be where we start.

Culture in society and in the broader business context is also changing. Advances in technology are opening up potential for enterprise, society and individuals. With that, data is fast becoming the lifeblood of successful organisations, both for profit and not for profit. Those that can capture, manage, analyse and make data an enabler for transformation have an opportunity to move ahead. Some of this change is positive: collaborative working and the power of utilising difference. But this evolution is slow and legacy thinking is still prevalent. We need to change the narrative. The legacy issues – silos, obsolete organisational culture, lack of agility – will persist unless we change the approach. The question is, are you ready to change?

The business environment has millions of ecosystems and your own organisation is one ecosystem created to solve a specific problem. Data evolution is needed to ensure we maximise value and create an environment that works in a complex and fast-moving world. Those who do not adjust to changes in cultural norms and ways of working, thinking and adopting technology in a positive way risk falling behind or becoming obsolete. The stark reality is that things need to change. Wrapping our heads around what we in business need to do to get ahead is critical to a sustainable and scalable future business. To do that, we need to manage cultural and behavioural change. We need to move fast, create simplicity and be pragmatic.

We and this book are here to help with this. By using a holistic approach based around ideas that can adapt, we will walk you through how you can lead change, connecting all the dependencies. We will also position how you can use a start-up approach to making data an enabler in an age when digital adoption is necessary for business and society to evolve.

Are you ready to evolve? Because data means business.

The primary purpose of this book is to create momentum around thinking about data differently. It is not meant as a step-by-step guide. We have pulled on our experiences of working with hundreds of organisations and thousands of people to provide approaches that have been successfully deployed, along with fundamental tools, methods and ideas. If you are ready to create change in your organisation, this book will help frame your thinking and put you on the path to success.

It will show how to create the right method for your organisation and ensure you have a clear alignment of the business strategy to your data strategy. It favours pragmatism over perfection, collaboration and cooperation over siloed thinking and business, and new ways of working over outdated data strategies and initiatives.

In this second edition, we have updated our concepts and frameworks as they have naturally matured and progressed during our time working with global organisations on their strategies, and as AI technology has exploded into the hands of consumers, employees, governments and the boardroom. This means the whole book has had an upgrade. The first edition was right for the time, this edition brings everything up to date.

Specifically, we have reviewed, improved and rewritten many sections, from culture to ethics, diversity to the history and future of the chief data officer (CDO) role. There is better clarity around how best to manage and govern your data, and we have improved the real examples we use to support the methods we discuss. Diagrams have been amended and sections moved to enhance the flow for you as a reader.

We have introduced new topics not covered previously around how to accelerate decision making, the use of business capabilities maps, the genesis, current status and future of AI, and we have included a clearer statement about the need for data and AI literacy. As with the first edition, we continue to aim to break down the complexity and demystify the confusion that so easily creeps in around data and AI. We clear the fog, so to speak.

This book is still for business leaders wanting to understand the best ways to get value from data and why data should be approached from a business context, not a technology one. It will help you to understand data's context within an organisation's ecosystem and how to create a culture of learning; it promotes insight-guided decision making and will help you keep your data strategy focused not on data but on your business. This book will help you level up your organisation so it can adapt, evolve and scale.

Like the first edition, this second edition is for CDOs and other data leaders looking to build their strategy and get early continual and sustained success. It will provide clear guidance on what to think about and how to start, scale and get the best results out of your data strategy for your business. Show it to your peers, leadership team and board so they 'get' what you are trying to achieve and how.

Finally, this book is for aspiring data leaders wanting to learn the breadth of challenge and opportunities required to be successful and who are ready to step up into that leadership position. It will help you level up your knowledge, business acumen, commercial awareness, leadership prowess and understanding of how your current role is fundamental to the success of your organisation.

This book is designed for you to dip into the relevant topics when you need to. Keep coming back to it to remind you of the tools and approaches. Use it to explain to others what you are trying to achieve and how. There are sections that frame mindset and concepts and others that walk through the journey you will need to go on, so you may also get value from working through each stage to make sure you haven't missed anything.

Part 1: Thinking Differently helps to frame the key concepts, lessons and mindsets required to be successful in modern digital business and in an innovative, progressive data and AI strategy. We also introduce the Level Up Framework, which shapes the stages discussed in Parts 2 and 3.

Part 2: Getting Off The Ground focuses on the early stages of your data journey and helps put organisation-wide roots down in a way that assures success. It explains how to create momentum, get the organisation behind the journey and build credibility.

Part 3: Growth And Impact helps you move out of thinking, planning and proofs of concept, to scale at pace and create an organisation guided by data. There are stories from some great organisations that have achieved success by applying data to everything they do.

Part 4: Defining And Delivering Your Strategy brings everything together to explain how to assess where you are and how to plan, build a data strategy and monitor progress. Here's where we cover the role of the CDO.

PART 1

THINKING DIFFERENTLY

The ability of an organisation to not only survive but thrive through good and challenging times is predicated on its ability to listen, learn and adapt; to build a culture that can not only handle change but has a thirst for it. Organisations that stand still run the risk of becoming obsolete. It may not happen overnight, but the world around you will chip away and eventually the inevitable will happen.

Once, Blockbuster was flying high; at its peak it had 9,000 stores globally and $5.9 billion in revenue, but the company missed the opportunity that online DVD rentals and then streaming presented to the industry.[1]

---

1   F Olito, 'The rise and fall of Blockbuster', *Business Insider* (20 August 2020), www.businessinsider.com/rise-and-fall-of-blockbuster, accessed 15 January 2025

The technology changed and their customers changed how they wanted to consume content. Blockbuster didn't pivot and missed the chance to continue to own the home movie consumption market. Enter Netflix and multiple other streaming services: Rakuten, Disney+, Prime Video... In 2000, Blockbuster turned down the opportunity to acquire Netflix for $50 million and with it the future in home entertainment. Once a darling on the high street, Blockbuster is now out of business.

Over the last few years, this Blockbuster/Netflix example has become something of a meme. Blockbuster runs an X account (x.com/blockbuster) where it pokes fun at itself for losing out to Netflix. There are, of course, many other examples of organisations being disrupted into bankruptcy – Kodak, once a giant in the photography industry, failed to transition to digital quickly enough. Toys R Us, the retailer loved by children for decades, couldn't compete with the likes of Amazon. Sears, once the largest US retailer, didn't keep up with changing consumer preferences.

The COVID pandemic created an incubator for entrepreneurs and innovators. Some disrupted, some did the disrupting. Clubhouse launched in 2020 and quickly gained popularity as an audio-only-based social networking app, disrupting the social media landscape. It rose to 17 million active monthly users within six months, gained a $4 billion valuation,[2] and then six months later lost 80% of its user base.[3]

While TikTok was launched earlier than Clubhouse, it saw explosive growth into the 2020s, massively changing the social media landscape. It has become a dominant platform for short-form video content, influencing trends, marketing strategies, and even the music industry. While it hasn't killed off other platforms in the way Netflix impacted Blockbusters, it's changed the game in many ways.

Dealing with change is challenging, but the change imperative is real. The way you think about change, the complexities and dependencies, makes or breaks your success. Consequently, this section shares ways to consider your business in the context of your critical capabilities, how they need to evolve, and how your data and AI strategy can and should directly support change.

It looks at business as an ecosystem and lessons we can learn from start-ups in how they test, evolve and iterate their value proposition. We explore people

---

2   K Zuritsky, 'What happened to Clubhouse? Next great social network has gone quiet', *Market Realist* (28 April 2023), https://marketrealist.com/company-industry-overviews/what-happened-to-clubhouse, accessed 15 January 2025

3   S Rao, 'The Airchat hype: but wait, what happened to Clubhouse?', *Medium* (19 April 2024), https://uxdesign.cc/what-happened-to-clubhouse-35228a6bbca4, accessed 15 January 2025

science and culture change as fundamental enablers. We consider the importance of ethics and diversity in your strategy. We introduce the idea of business capabilities as a tool for understanding your organisation, the need for data excellence, data products and services, and our Level Up Framework for starting and scaling your strategy.

ONE

A New Approach

The business ecosystem

On the African savannah there are thousands of life forms coexisting that are completely dependent on each other. Somehow, a correct balance is maintained. Water, air and grass are fundamental to the balance. Animal populations are estimated to have reduced by 70% in the last fifty years.[4]

---

4   A Kelley, 'Human activity has wiped out nearly 70 percent of
     the world's wildlife in just 50 years: report', Changing America
     (10 September 2020), https://thehill.com/changing-america/
     sustainability/environment/515808-human-activity-has-wiped-out-
     nearly-70-percent-of, accessed 15 January 2025

It is estimated that 99.9% of all species that have ever lived are extinct.[5] What does this have to do with data?

Despite all the hype, data is still not managed and used effectively. Without it an organisation could not survive, but like air it is taken for granted and assumed to be there. It is created in our processes, captured, digitised and may or may not be made available for decision making. Given the increasing understanding that data is a fundamental part of an organisation, we need to change how we think about it, not just in our organisation but in the wider business, economic and social environment.

Business is infinitely more complex. People are intricate and in our organisations we have created silos. We categorise and label behaviour, diversity, jobs and organisational structures, making the ecosystem hard to navigate. Culture is not something you can touch, yet it is an important part of getting an organisation to be data-guided. Using and managing data effectively is complex. Like the savannah, the business ecosystem is reliant on more than just the obvious factors. Gartner have defined eight variables for a business ecosystem: strategy, openness, participants,

---

5   C Wilcox, 'Human-caused extinctions have set mammals back millions of years', *National Geographic* (17 October 2018), www.nationalgeographic.com/animals/2018/10/millions-of-years-mammal-evolution-lost-news, accessed 15 January 2025

relationships, value exchange, industries, complexity and technology.[6]

James F Moore coined the term 'business ecosystem', which he described as a setting in which 'companies co-evolve capabilities around a new innovation: they work cooperatively and competitively to support new products, satisfy customer needs and eventually incorporate the next round of innovations.'[7] Thinking about business like an ecosystem is intended to drive innovation, growth and a more effective business.

This is only one version of what a business ecosystem is, but it demonstrates that if we are to implement the change needed to become a data-guided organisation we need to move away from thinking about data as special and separate. When implementing data, we need to use it to connect the organisation.

Business capability map

In the rapidly evolving landscape of modern business, organisations need to continuously adapt and refine their strategies to stay competitive. One powerful tool that supports this is the business capability map.

---

6   K Panetta, '8 dimensions of business ecosystems', Gartner (12 July 2017), www.gartner.com/smarterwithgartner/8-dimensions-of-business-ecosystems, accessed 15 January 2025

7   J Moore, 'Predators and prey: A new ecology of competition', *Harvard Business Review* (1999), 71(3): 75–86, https://hbr.org/1993/05/predators-and-prey-a-new-ecology-of-competition, accessed 15 January 2025

We like looking at an organisation through the context of its business capabilities as they not only help us to understand the business ecosystem, but they also allow us to better identify and prioritise the areas that can most benefit from applying data or AI. This leads us to better understand what data capabilities are needed, providing a helpful steer for the organisation's strategic priorities.

Unlike traditional process maps that focus on the how, business capability maps emphasise the what – what a company does and can do. Business capabilities are the ingredients of a business that give it the ability to deliver its products and/or services. They summarise the capacity, materials and expertise required to achieve the business objectives. By understanding the critical ingredients that make the organisation run, we can align responsibilities and understand dependencies. This allows for planning and prioritisation of resources to focus on what is important.

Business capability maps are also instrumental in long-term strategic planning. They help organisations identify gaps between current and future capabilities, enabling targeted investments and resource allocation. By providing a high-level view of what the business can achieve, these maps facilitate better decision making and strategic alignment.

There are some key characteristics of business capabilities:

- **Each capability cannot be repeated.** It is distinct. For example, you only have one sales capability.

- **A capability is not a reflection of the organisation structure.** For example, sales is a necessary capability that will be carried out by different teams, functions and departments.

- **Capabilities are descriptive.** It is not how something is done, but rather what is done. For example, a demand planning capability is something that requires input from manufacturing, operations, finance and product teams. The result of demand planning is having the right input for the manufacturing process to produce products as fast as possible to be able to sell more in line with customer demand.

- **Capabilities can be both tangible and intangible.** For example, manufacturing creates something tangible, but brand management creates something intangible.

- **Capabilities are outcome oriented.** Each capability needs a clear outcome. For example, business development might include client acquisition as its outcome.

What is important is creating something that is understood, described and agreed upon by your organisation. This map of the capabilities provides a consistent and transparent way for the organisation to understand what it does, and a way to instigate conversations between teams that is common, clear and understood.

The capabilities map is a great way to ensure that conversations around data and AI are focused on business outputs, not data outputs. It allows you to define what things mean and the context from different parts of the ecosystem. Over time, it also allows commonality of needs across the organisation to be understood, thereby increasing the value of the investments you make in the context of those needs.

For example, DataOps is a methodology used by data teams (we will discuss it later in the book). It is not something anyone outside the data team needs to understand per se, but it is important that the organisation as a whole understands that it is looking to deliver value fast, and that requires certain processes to be followed. That common understanding leads to positive results.

An example of a business capability map for a television manufacturing company might be:

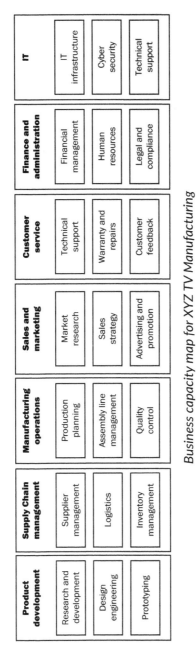

Business capacity map for XYZ TV Manufacturing

Product development	Supply Chain management	Manufacturing operations	Sales and marketing	Customer service	Finance and administration	IT
Research and development	Supplier management	Production planning	Market research	Technical support	Financial management	IT infrastructure
Design engineering	Logistics	Assembly line management	Sales strategy	Warranty and repairs	Human resources	Cyber security
Prototyping	Inventory management	Quality control	Advertising and promotion	Customer feedback	Legal and compliance	Technical support

We will show how you can use business capability maps as a way to target your data and AI strategy later in the book.

Culture and the science of people

Culture, like the broader business ecosystem, is not static; it evolves through a collective set of beliefs, values and attitudes. Culture has an impact on the strategic direction of the business and influences management decisions in all business functions. However, it is often not considered when we're looking at data.

Changing how you understand, manage and use data will influence the beliefs, values and attitudes of your organisation. What we have learned over the years is that no matter what the existing culture is in an organisation, if you want to embrace AI or improve your use of data, you will need to change your culture in some way.

Much is written about creating a data-driven culture or, as we prefer to call it, a data-guided culture. The focus is often on the data itself – how data is used, who uses it, what it's for. The organisation trains people in data and recruits new data people in the hope that the culture will change.

This misses the point. For an organisation to be guided by data and maximise the opportunities it presents, its people need to understand the culture and values of the business itself and marry those with the key cultural values needed to be a data-guided organisation.

Culture is organisation-wide, but within the organisation there are often subcultures. This helps create the silos that exist, which can lead to cultural problems. The culture is then used as an excuse for inefficiency. How often have you heard someone say, 'That's just the way we do it here'?

It's logical when we're thinking about data strategy that we should start by thinking about the business outcomes and the people needed to achieve results. Process defines the ways of working and is a point of reference for what is important and where to start. However, there is a danger in many organisations of starting not with understanding culture, but by implementing the next sexy thing – AI, anyone?

The thinking and ways of working brought into a business (and therefore the culture) are impacted heavily by the data industry itself, often detrimentally. The industry is awash with discussion, news, research, articles and focus on AI, deep learning, data science, statistics, predictions and algorithms. This is a world of science (or even science fiction) – a world where analytical and mathematical algorithms like linear regression, multivariate adaptive regression splines, neural networks and k-nearest neighbours are pointed at data and set to work.

This has led many organisations to make data science the heart of at least their thinking, if not their doing. In a world where facts and maths are used to infer, to learn, to devise probabilities and make predictions to recommend the right outfit, the right songs, the right hospital treatment, deliver the best advert, assess us for insurance risk and make ordering from Amazon even easier than it is now, the science of data is king – right?

Algorithms need data to learn. Creating algorithms that are not operationally effective, no matter how clever they are, will not bring true value. Data science is one of many components needed to maximise your understanding of what and how you operate. They can help simplify and automate decisions, but they need to exist in processes that touch real people and be managed and move with change in both the internal organisation and the external environment.

In this world of maths and data science, it is the science of people and the art of understanding and getting the best from those people that really impact the outcomes for most organisations. That's culture.

In her book *Weapons of Math Destruction*, Cathy O'Neil provides some great examples of AI models for good doing bad.[8] A strong culture built around creating models and validation of output in the right way is

---

8   C O'Neil, *Weapons of Math Destruction: How big data increases inequality and threatens democracy* (Crown Publishing Group, 2016)

critical if AI is to be a force for good. This does not just apply to AI, but to everything done across the organisation. Constructively challenging what you see and hear can only be achieved with the right culture.

Data science or people science? The clearer you are that integrating AI and making the best use of data is in fact as much about culture and your people as it is about process, technology and other factors that influence the overall business ecosystem, the better and quicker results you will see. Harnessing the science of people will help you drive your business forward and create an organisation guided by data.

When a start-up organisation begins, it is small and its people can make decisions fast. They can test and learn at pace, and get their products and services to the next phase of development quickly. They can easily collaborate. They can embed fresh thinking and behaviours into how they do things, without the baggage of legacy.

These things aren't always possible for established businesses. What is often not understood are the micro cultures that have built up over time and exist within teams, departments, functions and other collections of people in the organisation.

We have often heard the statement: 'That won't work in our business', but that's the point. Things won't work if the culture isn't in the right place, and to create the culture you require, you need to move away from fixed opinions and myths. By collaborating and working outside organisational norms, you will be influencing beliefs and attitudes.

You will need a level of organisational resilience to manage through change, but of course, you can't start by trying to change the entire business culture. You can, however, influence how the people behave and interact with each other bottom up and top down through mentoring and role modelling.

Culture change is ultimately driven by strong communication, leadership behaviours, education, collaboration, pragmatism, testing, learning and scaling what works, and connecting the components of the organisation's ecosystems. You change from within by starting small and then finding new ways to 'go viral'. By doing this, you are looking to create three key outcomes that drive you towards a data-guided culture:

1. Introduce core beliefs that data and AI can significantly and positively impact the organisation's outcomes.

2. Influence behaviours that support the culture you are trying to create.

3. Be an incubator for doing things differently and move away from the elements of the 'old' culture that are holding you back.

Everything is downstream from the culture you create, and we have seen huge gains being made by organisations that shift their culture. We have also seen large investments in technology go to waste because the required culture change around that technology to get the best use out of it wasn't considered or didn't happen.

Thinking about ethics and diversity

Two key components of driving change in business and society are:

- Better ethical decisions
- The ability to celebrate, understand and use the differences between people

Why be ethical? Nowadays, transparency and visibility are just a click away, so it is unlikely you can act unethically and avoid getting noticed. A recent example is the scandal involving Wirecard, a German payment processing company that disclosed a $2.3 billion accounting error, leading to the resignation and arrest of its CEO.[9] The scandal had an immediate impact on its stock price. While that can recover, it did cause long-term reputational damage, leading Wirecard to file for insolvency.

---

9   R Luke, 'The future of work: The 10 biggest company scandals in 2020', Ladders (1 February 2021), www.theladders.com/career-advice/the-10-biggest-company-scandals-of-2020, accessed 10 January 2025

There are numerous examples from the past of businesses acting in an unethical manner. In the 1940s and 1950s, cigarettes were marketed as good for your health. Companies even used doctors to reinforce the message in advertising. The cigarette industry at some point realised that this was not true, but despite knowing the health impacts of smoking, it continued to market cigarettes as safe.

Did you get into business to harm the environment, individuals or your employees? Of course not. How you react to new information can be the difference between acting ethically or unethically.

The way you embed ethical behaviour in your organisation is part of your culture. If it is not explicit, there will be an implicit cultural norm. Given the increased use of AI and algorithmic decision making, thinking about and planning around your moral compass in data is crucial.

Ethics and how you make decisions should be consistent in all parts of the organisation, so you need to consider your understanding of the culture around ethics. If the consistency is low then, like all things in business, you can use data as an enabler to help change the culture and process.

Ethics as it relates to data and AI has a number of considerations. People are concerned about how we use data, so it's important you ensure personal data is collected, stored and used responsibly. Equally, be clear about how data is used and how decisions made by AI improve transparency and build trust. Since data is used in AI models, and since historic data has potential for bias to be present, finding ways to avoid and mitigate bias to create fair and just outcomes becomes an ethical consideration.

Diversity, like ethics, has an increasing focus in society, and therefore in our organisations. In simple terms, diversity is about understanding and utilising the different experiences we have that shape us as individuals. By having varying viewpoints on problems, you can ensure that input in your organisation is not one-dimensional.

However, diversity is a lot more complex than skin colour or sexual orientation. To effect change, you need to have an organisation that truly embraces difference and uses it to effectively solve problems.

Managing diversity is not easy, but there are benefits for the organisation: it forces change and provides an opportunity for people to evaluate their previous bias. Take the example of hiring people with autism into your team. High-functioning people with autism may require you to change the working environment and the way you manage individuals. How you instruct people and the work itself will need to be thought through to ensure you have happy and productive employees and an approach that works for everyone.

Diversity in data and AI is crucial for several reasons. Diverse teams help identify and mitigate biases in AI algorithms thanks to broader perspectives, leading to fairer outcomes. These varied perspectives enhance problem solving and innovation by breaking free from echo-chamber and group think. Ensuring diverse data sets helps AI systems serve a broader range of users more equitably.

Diversity is about being able to manage and understand difference to drive real change. Like ethics, diversity needs a broad approach and to be consistently applied. The diversity wheel below highlights the many components of diversity and indicates why bias can and does exist when teams are less inclusive and made up of similar individuals with a limited range of characteristics. As individuals, we are not one-dimensional; like an ecosystem, we have multiple inputs that make us who we are.

Regardless of any regulation, it makes sense to change the way we drive more ethical and inclusive behaviour, use data and understand why the differences between us can make both business and broader society a better place. For sure, profit is still fundamental, but a better balance is needed to create real value, and more flexible and inclusive organisations as society and business evolve.

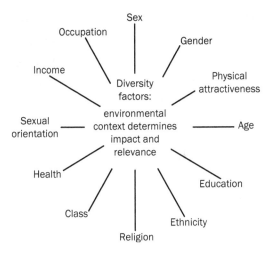

Human diversity characteristics

Having the organisational awareness and conscience around ethics and diversity encourages you to do this. Developing risk frameworks gives people the principles, policies and standards that are expected. Regular audits and monitoring offer you the tools needed to ensure compliance and course correct challenges.

Diversity advocate and thought leader Kim Gray summarises this nicely for us:

'Diversity, equity and inclusion (DEI) should be an important strategic consideration for talent acquisition, management and building a positive culture. This isn't a nice to have but a critical component that builds a real sense of belonging for staff within the organisation. It's key to building a great place to work and a driving force behind joint collaboration and stronger relationships across teams. Never has this been a more important topic than in the building of products and services, AI driven or otherwise, that represent organisations' diverse customer base.'[10]

Data, AI and decisions

Data means business, business means data.

Making and executing decisions is the bread and butter of business leaders, operators and workers across the world. Where to deploy resources? How should we invest our money? What should I offer this customer who is about to leave us? How do I get charitable donations from more members? Who are our customers and how do I retain them? How do I maximise capital? What are the chances of success in our targeted regions? How do we balance adding value to the shareholders, employees and society? Every day, there are decisions to be made that have huge consequences.

To help answer these questions, make decisions and deliver results, organisations create a vision, set their strategy and allocate money and resources to implementing day-to-day operations, changes and strategic objectives. They get their teams behind that strategy, execute it and then try to track how they are performing. In the best case everything is successful;

---

10 Interview with Kim Gray, 14 November 2024

in the worst case they fail as a business. The business environment is becoming increasingly complex with supply chain vulnerability, geopolitical risk and variable availability of capital and skills.

Heraclitus, a Greek philosopher, argued that change is the only constant.[11] We add to that: 'Uncertainty is the only thing we're certain of.' We cannot plan for or know what's coming all the time. We can only set ourselves up to deal with that uncertainty and be able to respond. In his book *Management: Tasks, responsibilities, practices*, Peter Drucker argued that strategic planning and innovation should be carried out on the basis that the future is uncertain and unpredictable.[12]

Since we cannot predict what will happen, it's about getting better at taking the right risks rather than removing them completely. We need to embrace change, embrace uncertainty and set ourselves up accordingly.

Our basic human need is to feel like we belong, that we are part of something special and exciting. Increasingly this means fair pay for our work and a recognition that what we do has value to our customers and society. We are looking for a trend of positive outcomes: more successes than failures, more upsides

---

11 Stanford Encyclopedia of Philosophy, 'Heraclitus' (3 September 2019), https://plato.stanford.edu/entries/heraclitus, accessed 15 January 2025
12 P Drucker, *Management: Tasks, responsibilities, practices* (Taylor & Francis, 1973)

than downsides, more predictability in outcomes than shooting in the dark, and better management through uncertain, changing times.

Data is the enabler that will help us achieve this outcome. That's it. It's about helping to plan better, react faster, manage through ambiguity, listen and learn concisely, get more consistency, make decisions consciously and thoughtfully. It's about better understanding your failures and your successes and applying that learning to get better next time. If you can do all these things, you win, but winning requires a consistent approach to solving root cause problems.

Data is a business skill. A big, critical, value-adding, differentiating skill. Like understanding budgets, managing people, procuring products and services and engaging with partners, the skill of data is something that you and your team must develop for getting and staying ahead. Data is a business profession. The industry tends to use the phrase 'data literacy' and this is essentially what it means – an organisation that is able to apply insights to a business situation in order to make better decisions. Getting value out of data is therefore everyone's responsibility. Data means business.

Dr Beatrice Lafon, Chair and Non-Executive Director at a number of consumer facing organisations and ex Chief Executive Officer at Claire's, Pimkie, Kondor, Etam Group and T J Hughes, has much experience in making big strategic and operational decisions to drive growth and efficiencies and says:

'Innovation and resilience have long been the code words for lasting business success. In the digital age, data (think data points, data science, data infrastructure) has become a core capability to support and indeed at times drive both innovation and resilience.

Historically, a business would have looked to financial data as a key driver of decision making. New data points now exist such as customer data, employee data, supplier data, product data, all of which can support excellence in decision making.

Data points on their own have very little value. However, it is possible to transform those data points into insights by making the information reliable, timely, relevant, connected and actionable. As a business leader, it is not data you need, it is insights. You need to be able answer the 'So what?' question, and quickly. Today, we can easily combine Data with AI, and that can become your secret sauce to strategic decisions and operational excellence.'

Creating the data-guided business

It's important to create a business that has data at the centre of all decision making. Decision making on strategy development, operational execution, reaction to internal or external events and engaging with your stakeholders. It won't always make the decisions for you, but through a combination of human smarts, intuition and leadership guided by the insights and learning that data gives you, it will produce better decisions more often, and provide the ability to assess the impact of those decisions.

The evolution of where and how data is maximised in your business fundamentally shifts the return you get from the investments in using data. Your use of data and how pervasive it is, in decision making specifically, determines how data-guided you can be. The diagram below shows the states you can be in with regard to the pervasiveness of data for decision making.

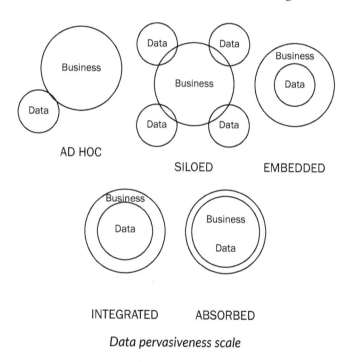

Data pervasiveness scale

Since data is an enabler and a way to connect the organisation together, you want to move away from a place where data is not used by the business to drive the agenda. It should not be seen as separate, outside the day job and for someone else to deal with. It should not be ad hoc and held or managed in silos. It needs to move to a place where the use, activation and change made through data should be pervasive and seamless with the job of your teams. It is about being embedded, integrated and absorbed into how you operate.

Major market events like pandemics, wars, oil price changes, interest rate adjustments and government policy have shown us that the ability to adapt is critical for survival. Even if you want to be a 100% digital business, you still need to operate in an ecosystem where not everything can be done digitally.

If you want to be a data-guided business, you will need to know what data is needed, create processes to digitise inputs and understand what and how you operate, think, behave and what impact the external ecosystem has on your organisation. Data-guided and digitally savvy businesses exist, but they are the exception, not the rule. There are organisations that use data effectively to set strategy, manage operations, engage with customers and judge performance. Think of Netflix, Facebook, Uber. Think of online marketplaces like Amazon, ASOS and Alibaba. They are data and digital native. They have grown up striving for and succeeding in having data absorbed into their operations, processes and decision making.

Many organisations continue to operate in a manner that does not adopt digital and data in the most effective way, generally because of the legacy that has been created, but also because of old mindsets and inertia. Data is still not embraced, embedded, integrated or absorbed due to the large amount of change needed. Change is hard.

The lucky few that get to a point where data is absorbed into the fabric of the business can state they are a data-guided organisation and can act like the digital and data natives of this world. They will see the consistent incremental benefit that operating in this way has and gain considerable competitive advantage over others. And they too need to continue to evolve and be set up to do this effectively.

The data value chain

What do we mean by data? Ask a room full of people what data is and you will get a different answer from everyone. Some will talk about a report they get, some will talk about the attributes captured in a customer relationship management (CRM) database, some will talk about the output of an algorithm, some will say it's what Facebook collects, some may even say it's something they get with their phone contract so they can watch Netflix and TikTok.

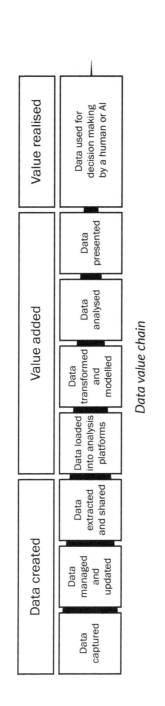

Data value chain

Value realised

Data used for decision making by a human or AI

Value added

Data presented

Data analysed

Data transformed and modelled

Data loaded into analysis platforms

Data created

Data extracted and shared

Data managed and updated

Data captured

Data ambiguity creates a challenge in terms of under-standing what problem we are solving. Getting the most value from data requires us to understand it at all stages of its lifecycle and value chain. How many times have you heard that data is out of scope for a project? How many times have you heard the term 'data' used in multiple different contexts in a meeting? How many times have you heard: 'Why don't we have the data we need?'

The answer is that data can mean different things to different people depending on the stage of the data value chain they are referring to, often without them knowing. The diagram above shows this value chain and why different interpretations exist.

1. Data is created.
   - Data is captured in systems either by humans manually entering it (eg a website sign-up form, creating a new record in your CRM system or creation of a new product in your product management system), or automatically by a system (eg the time you spend looking at a social media post, your vehicle registration being captured by a city camera or your satellite navigation system capturing where you have travelled).
   - Data is managed in that system (eg customer records are enhanced with new attributes, financial transactions are adjusted, notes are

added to records, social media topics you interact with are grouped).

– Data is extracted from those source systems (eg moving customer data from the CRM system into your email campaign engine) or shared with others for the purposes of adding value or managing a downstream process.

2. Data has value added to it – it can be uploaded to a data and analytics platform, transformed through aggregation, consolidation, calculation, manipulation, then analysed to find insights, answers, trends and patterns. It will be presented to a human for interpretation (eg via a report, dashboard or alert) or a system for further use and processing (eg to an AI model).

3. The value of the data is realised – the use of the data should drive an action (eg changing an email campaign, fixing a broken process, launching a new product) that aims to change outcomes and realise value. This may be by a human manually making a decision and taking that action (eg choosing a new product feature or new market to launch in), or by a machine automating a decision that drives some change (eg what content to serve to someone on an app or how to allocate stock to high street stores).

At all these stages, data can be classed as 'the data', so it's important to recognise these different lenses and, more importantly, the increasing value that data has as it passes through this value chain.

AI has landed

The CEO at one of our car manufacturing clients recently said that they expect AI to have the same impact on their customer services as robotics had on manufacturing. Robotics have allowed 50% more vehicles to be produced, a 20–30% increase in manufacturing efficiency, and reduced defects and rework, increasing quality. The number of people the client required halved overnight when robotics were introduced and since then, hundreds of thousands fewer people have been required. That's one heck of a shift and a very high expectation.

AI has made a significant impact in boardrooms in the past few years, which has sparked a mix of excitement, confusion and appetite. And its impact has been felt beyond the boardroom too. Your teams are using AI daily to improve their social posts and writing, your kids are using it for their homework, your parents are using it for recipes and to write a letter to the local council, and software providers are embedding it wherever they can into their platforms. It's made such an impact that Jack Ma, founder and chairman at Alibaba, said 'In thirty years, a robot will likely be on the cover of *Time* Magazine as the best CEO',[13] while China-based NetDragon Websoft already says it is the first company in the world to appoint an AI as

---

13 S Pham, 'Jack Ma: In 30 years, the best CEO could be a robot', *CNN Business* (24 April 2017), https://money.cnn.com/2017/04/24/technology/alibaba-jack-ma-30-years-pain-robot-ceo/index.html, accessed 10 January 2025

its CEO.[14] This transformative technology has landed and it's predicted to continue to impact the world as much as the car and the internet did, if not more.

It's strange, though, as modern AI has been around for a long time. In 1950, Alan Turing published the paper 'Computing machinery and intelligence' where he proposed his now famous Turing Test to determine if a machine can exhibit intelligent behaviour indistinguishable from a human.[15] In 1966, computer scientist Joseph Weizenbaum developed ELIZA, an early natural language processing program that simulated conversation. There was huge excitement over the technology and its capabilities, but through the 1970s, 1980s and into the 1990s, there was reduced funding and interest in the research due to unmet expectations. This period became known as the 'AI winter'.

With advances in machine learning (ML), neural networks and computational power, there was renewed interest, and then breakthrough research in the 2000s. This has ramped up with huge investment being allocated in academia, governments and corporates. Since then, AI algorithms have proliferated and are being used to assess fraud and risk by banks, to personalise marketing content by retailers, to search

---

14   A Cuthbertson, 'Company that made an AI its chief executive sees stocks climb', *Independent* (16 March 2023), www.independent. co.uk/tech/ai-ceo-artificial-intelligence-b2302091.html, accessed 10 January 2025

15   A Turing, 'Computing machinery and intelligence' (*Mind*, 1950)

photos on your phone, and to route calls by voice in customer contact centres.

In November 2022, the game changed again with the release of ChatGPT 3.0 by OpenAI. It's in the category of AI called generative AI (GenAI). While previous AI models mainly dealt with tasks typically associated with the left side of the human brain – logic, sequence, linear thinking, mathematics and facts – this technology is capable of tasks associated with the right side of the human brain – imagination, arts, creativity, holistic thinking, non-verbal cues. It honestly felt a bit like magic when it was first released and many still look on in shock and awe.

Its growth from there has been explosive. OpenAI acquired 1 million users within the first five days of launching in November 2022.[16] Compare this to other well-known fast-growing companies – Instagram took 2.5 months, Netflix took around 3.5 years. By April 2024, ChatGPT was getting close to 2 billion visits each month. The shift this has created across industries has been immense.

Klarna is a prime example of this shift. The company has embraced AI in a big way, particularly with its AI assistant, which now handles two-thirds of customer service chats, and it plans on removing 7,000 customer

16 F Duarte, 'Number of ChatGPT users (Dec 2024)', *Exploding Topics* (3 December 2024, updated 4 February 2025), https://explodingtopics. com/blog/chatgpt-users, accessed 10 January 2025

contact representatives.[17] This assistant has improved efficiency, handling tasks like refunds and returns, and even fostering healthy financial habits.

Klarna's CEO, Sebastian Siemiatkowski, has high-lighted the profound impact AI is having on the company's operations.[18,19] He mentions that AI is not just about improving customer experiences, but also about creating more interesting challenges for employees and better returns for investors. This reflects the broader appetite and excitement in the boardroom for AI's potential to transform business operations.

While exciting, this rapid adoption also brings confusion and challenges. Companies must navigate the complexities of building and integrating AI, while ensuring it aligns with their own goals and values. Getting this mix of impact and careful adoption correct will be the difference between success and failure. You and your organisation should embrace this challenge now as the train has already left the station. This book, with its frameworks and

---

17 Klarna, 'AI assistant handles two-thirds of customer service chats in its first month' (27 February 2024), www.klarna.com/international/press/klarna-ai-assistant-handles-two-thirds-of-customer-service-chats-in-its-first-month, accessed 10 January 2025

18 'Klarna CEO on AI Role, IPO plans, boardroom drama', YouTube (8 March 2024), www.youtube.com/watch?v=7_dXx8arTc0, accessed 10 January 2025

19 Klarna, '90% of Klarna staff are using AI daily – game changer for productivity' (14 May 2024), www.klarna.com/international/press/90-of-klarna-staff-are-using-ai-daily-game-changer-for-productivity, accessed 10 January 2025

approaches, provides a structured and consistent way to approach data and AI.

One final consideration for the changes AI will inevitability bring. With all the hype around AI, it would be easy to think that since it can support us in so many ways, we will be able to think less. The opposite is true – we need to avoid outsourcing our thinking to AI.

Leaders and users of AI need to be more thoughtful, more analytical and more challenging. It is important we can consider results from AI systems, discern biases and realise what's fact and what's false, so that we understand the impact these results have on the decisions we, and indeed AI, need to make. This means we need to think, learn and behave differently if we are to truly get the exponential benefit AI promises.

A start-up philosophy

This is not another trendy metaphor. This is a philosophy we suggest you adopt to help facilitate the change needed to embed data into the DNA of your organisation. There is a lot to learn from the mindset used in successful start-ups that move out of those early stages and grow exponentially for incredible results.

Let's start by describing some key attributes of start-ups that you can use in developing the way you approach your strategy:

- They have an idea that is new and innovative.

- They aim to solve a problem when there is no obvious alternative.

- Success is not guaranteed and requires entrepreneurial thinking and leadership.

- In the early stages, a start-up is small and has not yet developed a scalable product or service.

- Start-ups use speed and design as a key differentiator.

- They use legacy to their advantage and as a catalyst for change.

- They use an approach that lets them test an idea, learn from it and only scale the things that are working.

- They build an early version of their product or service, often called a minimum viable product (MVP), which has the minimum required to add value and test the proposition.

- They do not have long-term funding and need to prove value to get funding, survive and thrive.

- They are drivers of innovation and change.

There are plenty of excellent books on the subject of start-ups. Eric Ries's *The Start-Up Way* is a good example if you want to learn more about how to apply the start-up mentality and approach in organisations more generally.[20]

We are not saying your organisation should actually be a start-up, but the philosophy and attributes we've mentioned are important. It's about adaptability, pragmatism, testing and learning, listening and reacting to customers appropriately. Often in organisations, the culture stymies employees in acting differently. Our approach is based around treating the things you do with data, and increasingly AI, like you are taking new products or services to market.

Data is prevalent in everything your organisation does. The issue of how to manage data and bring value is a holistic one. Adopting this approach to data allows you to change the culture from the inside with real behaviours and ensure you show progress in a developing, positive way.

You can use this approach regardless of your organisation's maturity. It is fundamentally about changing how you look at and use data. This means being innovative, thinking differently and solving problems pragmatically.

You can apply this approach to the development of any solution, but let's take a simple example at this stage. In the real world, you're usually trying to solve

20 E Ries, *The Start-Up Way: How entrepreneurial management transforms culture and drives growth* (Portfolio, 2017)

problems that are causing your organisation some pain, and often you have a hypothesis of why. Each time you find out your hypothesis is wrong, you can increment the next step in solving your business issue. This is about understanding a problem and breaking down a way to solve it in a positive, pragmatic manner.

Let's assume, for example, that you find some of your product margins are much lower than you expect compared to the other products in the same category. You ask, 'Should we stop selling these products?'

When you look at the underlying issue, it turns out that the cost data for the product is being entered manually by multiple individuals in different locations. There is no clear definition for the values being entered to calculate the margin, and the choices are confusing when you're setting up the product. The product type 'other' is therefore the default selection individuals are using when they don't know what else to enter.

You can solve this problem like a start-up, or you can put together a long, weighty capital-expenditure-requiring programme, with a business case and drawn-out approvals. We say approach it like a start-up: put together a small team with members from different parts of the organisation who have the required knowledge to contribute – product, finance and data. They design something small, maybe in

Excel, and validate that the output fits into the broader solution. It is then iterated until it is good enough (not perfect) to ensure there is clarity on the product margin of the products sold.

It wouldn't have the rigour of a fully blown solution, but would form the basis of an ongoing solution. This whole process would be done quickly, collaboratively and iteratively to build something just good enough to solve your business issue.

The underlying problem in this example is one of definition, data quality, reference data and process, as opposed to an actual issue with product margins. This test and learn approach allows you to spot that underlying problem before making the big decision to stop selling the products. It also means you have a clear understanding of what a product's actual margin is and can make informed decisions about product development or retirement from the portfolio.

Introduction to data and AI products and services

The benefit of thinking about data as a product or service is that it forces the user to answer the questions:

- What do I want to do with the data?

- What is the outcome I am after?

- What is involved in getting my need solved?

- What support do I need?

As mentioned earlier, the problem with the term 'data' is that it has multiple meanings depending on context. The concept of data products and services has been around for a while but it is difficult to implement unless you have a holistic approach to making data an enabler. 'I can't get the data I need' can mean an issue with access to a system, the data may not be available, or the data is not well defined and therefore is not available. 'The data is wrong' could mean that the filters used to produce the report have led to an unexpected outcome, or the answer interpreted from the data is not what the user wants to hear. 'The data quality is poor' could mean the source of the data is incomplete, or that the meaning of the data is not consistent and understood. 'I need the data' could mean an excel data dump, a report or data available in a data warehouse. Instead of talking about data, we must change the narrative to understand what we need to do with data, to meet a business outcome.

The business needs to become data-guided. To achieve this, everyone should be able to communicate what they need from data. You don't do this by talking about 'data'; you do it by ensuring everyone can use data effectively in whatever role they have in the organisation. To do this we will define what users need from data with a set of products and services.

This allows users to clearly understand what they need from the data and will help the data literacy improve over time. The products and services concept is the method we will use to change the narrative, create agility, focus on measurable outcomes and deliver results with pace.

Data and AI products

As citizens and consumers, we interact with products and services all the time. These can be digital products like Spotify and Netflix; physical products like bread, televisions, shoes; or hybrid products that blend physical and digital such as Amazon or Uber where you engage with a digital product (an app in this instance) to get access to a physical product or service.

Products usually exist to solve a customer need. You want to listen to music or watch a movie, you are hungry so you need some food or you're going for a run so need a pair of trainers. The product has been created to satisfy that need. Each product will have many features including its cost, its uses, where it can be stored, how long it lasts, the sizes it comes in, the people you can share it with and so on depending on the product. Individual products can also be used as part of another product and the value of the finished good is greater than the value of any of the individual ingredients.

The company that provides that product will have metrics (or key performance indicators, KPIs) to assess the performance of that product – number of products sold, monthly active users, monthly recurring revenue, stock holding, profitability, units in transit, customer satisfaction score, value of wastage and so on. These metrics tell the company how that product is performing and should guide it towards how to improve the performance or whether it is time to retire it in favour of new and better products.

Each of the products generated or services provided by the company will be owned by someone. They act as the manager for that product and are measured on its success. While different industries have different names for this role, they are essentially the product manager.

In digital teams, this is a common role and is usually broken down into components of the overall product. For example, at Spotify there may be a different product manager for the 'discover weekly' product than there will be for the 'sign up' product. Fast-moving consumer goods (FMCG) companies like Unilever and Procter & Gamble have brand managers or product managers who oversee the development, marketing and performance of specific products or brands within the company's portfolio.

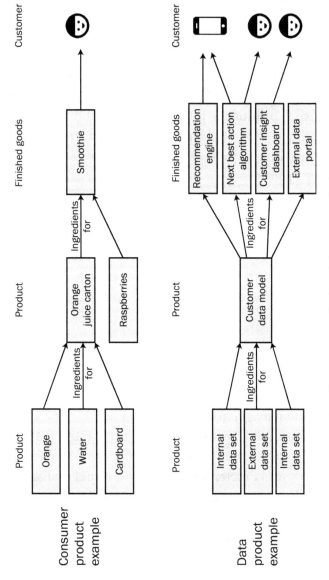

Consumer product vs data as a product

There are proven benefits of treating data and AI as a product in your organisation in a similar way to physical and digital products. You will see in the figure above a comparison between the products used to create a smoothie (finished good) and those used to create a data product, for example a dashboard, or an AI product, for example a recommendation engine or an algorithm (finished goods), to show how the concept of a consumer product can be applied to a data or AI product.

These are all examples of products that you could build to support business outcomes. Some are purely data-based products, some are AI driven:

- Transaction enrichment product

- Customer service bot

- Manual process automation

- Sales dashboard

- Pricing optimisation engine

- Predictive model

- Data extraction process

- Recommendation engine

Some of these products are there to serve as ingredients for other products and some are finished goods in their own right. Like the consumer products mentioned, each product:

- Exists to solve a customer need

- Has features and benefits

- Has key performance indicators (KPIs)

- Has a product manager who owns the features, benefits and is measured on the KPIs

While each data product may be in the same technology ecosystem, the underlying technology used to create the product may be different. For example, the technology you use to create a sales dashboard will be different to the technology you use to build a predictive model. Each data product can have one or many uses and ways of people and systems accessing said product. A recommendation engine might be accessed by its output being served up to a website so the customer sees personalised products in real time. It may also provide an output that creates relevant recommendations in an outbound email campaign. This is just like the smoothie in the example. That smoothie could be bought from a shop, a kiosk, a vending machine or in a restaurant.

CDO at Aramisauto in France, Anne-Claire Baschet, says:

> 'Often the main priority for data leaders is focused around adoption. This is predicated on building something like a data warehouse, a reporting solution or algorithm and then working hard to try and get the assumed end customer of that to use it.

Convincing people to adopt a solution becomes the focus, not solving the customer need. Instead, the management of data as a product starts with the problem that users have and are trying to solve and then prioritises working in collaboration with the end customer on a data product that is needed. The person you are building for is baked into the answer, they want it.'[21]

Treating data as a product requires a new way of thinking, new approaches to delivering data solutions and new roles to manage your outputs. We cover this through the book to help you embed this mentality and approach.

Data and AI services

Service is taking often intangible action to create value for someone else. That action is the experience, expertise and understanding required to build and serve data and AI products. This is usually the role of a specialist data team or teams. They are helping to federate data capability into the organisation through the defined set of services created to solve the business needs.

While data and AI products should be accessible and consumable, it is important to understand that a product may need some services to be useful or be

---

21 Interview with Anne-Claire Baschet, 29 November 2020

part of an overall data and AI offering inside your business. Let's use the example of data quality. The data quality service includes data profiling, quality assessment, monitoring and reconciliation, and finally remediation. We have labelled it a service because there is a need for someone to provide expert advice, guidance and training and to help create data quality rules for the business.

Data profiling allows the business to understand the data and focus on the attributes that may need attention. Let's say your business outcome is ensuring the address of the customer is correct. You will ideally use a data quality profile dashboard, for example (a data product). The activity of setting up the tool and training the business user how to profile their data is an example of the service in support of that product. If all fields in the address are of good quality except postcode then you focus on defining how to fix postcode. Profiling has allowed you to narrow the scope of the activity needed to meet the business outcome of a valid customer address.

The quality assessment may include reviewing the process, defining critical data, looking to identify owners and determining any data which may need profiling completed. These activities need someone who can run workshops, interpret business jargon and understand how ownership works. This is a pure service offering.

Monitoring will likely be undertaken by providing a dashboard (data product) with regular updates and thresholds to ensure whatever business context the data is used for is fit for purpose. This will be an ongoing activity, undertaken by a business user who should be self-sufficient, ie can access their dashboards and identify action needed to ensure their business outcome is met. The data service will be in place to support that monitoring should it extend outside the remit of that particular business user.

By using a combination of products and services, we can ensure that we improve a business outcome; with ownership in place, we have increased accountability and documented a key process so it can be simplified or at a minimum understood and maintained. The business users utilise data products and services to be independent from a central data team for day-to-day activities. We are effectively federating out data responsibility in the business, which is becoming data-guided.

In the smoothie example, a service could be delivering the raw materials. It could be training and servicing the commercial blender so the shop can make and sell the smoothie. The key point here is that data services and products are often synergistic. This is especially true in the data space where the value is in a combined set of services and products.

Introducing the Level Up Framework

Having worked with hundreds of organisations across the private, public and third sectors, we have clearly seen that certain activities are consistently required to create the kind of success that the data and AI 'brand' promises. Time and again we have seen the same blockers and challenges inhibiting organisations from meeting expectations. There is frustration and anxiety from business leaders about what to do first, which order to proceed in, how quickly to progress certain elements and how to make success more certain. While every situation is different, there is commonality in the building blocks and activities that are required as you progress to becoming an organisation that is truly data-guided.

The Level Up Framework is a method we have developed to make the journey more practical, more predictable and easier to explain. It removes the fog and brings clarity to what you need to do, in what order and to what end. The framework values business outcomes and building capabilities in equal measure but prioritises an approach that focuses (to the point of obsession) on adding incremental business value. It has taken learning from the start-up philosophy and digital native organisations and applied these through the lens of the data journey.

The Level Up Framework is based on five broad stages that provide activities to carry out and the criteria that tell you when you are ready to go to the next stage. Each stage builds on the last and, the better you achieve the criteria of one stage, the more certain and likely you are of success in the subsequent stage. This book breaks down these stages, giving clarity about what you should be thinking about, what you should be doing and how best to punch through to the next stage.

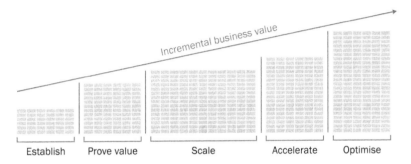

The Level Up Framework

Here are the stages of the framework:

- **Stage 1 – Establish:** set the agenda for data and AI in your organisation, get buy-in and initial funding. Optimum duration: three to six months. Educate the organisation:
    - Identify the business needs for data and impact of AI
    - Create a starter team
    - Build the case and get initial investment
    - Communication and collaboration

- **Stage 2 – Prove Value:** build excitement, buzz, credibility, and prove the value of data and AI by delivering business return, building foundational capabilities and refining the roadmap. Optimum duration: three to six months.

  - Build a data and AI product that delivers small value

  - Create visibility of core business metrics

  - Establish technology practice

  - Get investment to scale

  - Communication and collaboration

- **Stage 3 – Scale:** deliver business value at scale across the organisation and cement your core capabilities. Optimum duration: six to twelve months. Deliver big business returns.

  - Scale data and AI products and services

  - Grow skills and organisation design

  - Mature the operating model

  - Embed data-guided culture

  - Communication and collaboration

- **Stage 4 – Accelerate:** shorten the time to market for business outcomes at scale through data and AI products and services. Optimum duration: value-driven. Deliver fast business returns.

  - Build strategic optimum organisation

  - Implement event-driven and automated actions

- Incremental, rapid innovation
- Continuous improvement/learning

- **Stage 5 – Optimise:** refine and optimise processes, outcomes and results. Optimum duration: ad infinitum. Focus on optimisation of process and outcomes.
  - Think small adjustments, huge returns
  - Hands-free decision making
  - Valued data asset
  - No decisions made without data

Ultimately these stages create the necessary journey for you and your organisation. Graeme McDermott, CDO at Tempcover (and formerly Addison Lee and the AA), encapsulates this nicely having spent thirty years in the industry:

'The data profession often attracts a variety of "segments" or personas, one of the most recognised being the meticulous, detail-oriented and precision-driven data analyst. I'll admit, I've been (and sometimes still am) part of that group. The challenge comes when you're handed data that doesn't meet the standards you'd set for yourself. Ironically, when data professionals share their own data, it often feels like a military operation, every detail checked and rechecked to perfection.

This mindset, while admirable, can create a paralysing cycle of striving for unattainable perfection. The reality is, trying to achieve flawless data in one go can feel like boiling the ocean; a task so monumental that it risks burnout or abandonment.

What I've learned is that data is not a destination, it's a journey. Along that journey, you need to identify and aim for smaller, achievable waypoints. These interim goals make the process manageable and ensure progress, allowing you to reflect on and celebrate how far you've come.

In today's world, this philosophy is more relevant than ever. As businesses increasingly embrace AI, the quality of data becomes paramount to achieving meaningful outcomes. AI is only as good as the data it's trained on, and imperfect or incomplete data will lead to flawed insights and decisions. By focusing on incremental improvements and embracing the journey of data refinement, we ensure that the data fuelling AI initiatives is not just good, but transformative for the business.'[22]

---

22 Interview with Graeme McDermott, 3 January 2024

PART 2

GETTING OFF THE GROUND

Like a new boss at a sports club who lays out their vision for the club, the style of play they want to create, the expectations they have of their team, the way they treat the support staff and the communication and passion they build with the fans, the early stages of your journey are critical to your success or failure. Don't underestimate the importance of getting off on the right foot and its impact on your ability to drive business value.

Building strong foundations will provide you with a clear message about your intentions to create standout value from data. Get this stage right and you will set yourself up much better than those who jump straight to hiring twenty data scientists, buying the most expensive technology on the market and trying to implement the latest ML.

In this section we cover the first two stages of the Level Up Framework: Establish the Agenda and Prove Value. As in the early stages of a start-up, you'll be understanding your customers, building your community, defining your proposition, assessing your market fit, securing early investment, building credibility, proving value to your customers and stakeholders and educating your audience on the upsides of this journey.

At the end of each of the first four stages of the Level Up Framework, we also share what we call the 'breakthrough criteria', which act as a guide on what you should achieve by the end of each stage to punch through to the next stage successfully.

TWO

Establish The Agenda

Let's get something clear. You aren't doing this for the sake of it. You aren't doing it because you read in *The Economist* that 'data is the new oil' (it isn't by the way). You aren't doing it because your neighbour at a barbecue told you how they delivered ten times the return from implementing some artificial intelligence into their marketing funnel. You aren't doing it for fear of missing out (FOMO). These factors may be motivators but they aren't your main reasons.

You are doing this for real meaningful and transformational impact for you, your business, your shareholders, your stakeholders, your employees and, most importantly, the customers that your organisation serves. As Ellie Norman, chief marketing officer at Formula E and previously at Manchester United and Formula 1, states:

> 'Data is the heart of modern marketing. When you mix it with AI, you get this amazing ability to really get what customers want, spot trends, and craft strategies that drive engagement and growth. It's not just about gathering data; it's about turning it into insights and using generative AI to spark creativity and improve pace. It's like having a superpower for innovation!'[23]

The mindset needed during this stage is all about understanding the impact data and AI can have and how that aligns itself to your business goals. It's about creating desire and excitement about how much better things can be if you use data effectively in your decision making. You need to be thinking like a leader. You're campaigning. You're setting out your aspirations. Most importantly, you're listening. You're collaborating and being consultative. You're out building business relationships with the people who own the key metrics of the business and those that can influence those metrics.

Visionary leadership is needed to build excitement, momentum, desire and a thirst for business growth through the use of data and analytics. The board needs to hear how this impacts the future of the company and

---

23 Interview with Ellie Norman, 2 November 2024

its outcomes. Department heads need to know how their world will be impacted if they apply data to it.

Think about a brand that you love. Nike. Apple. Brewdog. Your local coffee shop. You're behind them, right? You love what they do, how they do it, what they stand for. You get them. You tell your friends about them. You feel part of the community. This is the mindset needed and the brand you want to create around the agenda you want to put in place.

This stage, establishing the agenda, is exactly that. It's getting clarity about the opportunity for the organisation, developing an understanding of how well set up the business is to achieve that opportunity and creating an agile and iterative plan for what is required.

This chapter is going to give you clarity over the way you establish that agenda, with pace and certainty, to build your solid foundations.

It's a bit of a mess: Managing data

The funny thing about data is that even if you haven't consciously or strategically tried to sort it out before, it's still likely that huge investment has already been made in it.

Think about your finance department and the hours spent pulling spreadsheets together to report on figures for the board. Think about the marketing team, who have invested in a third party to cobble together some of your customer data and apply it with external data to help build insight. How about the operations team, who hire people to build reports to help understand broken processes? Don't forget the customer services team, who are buying data from an agency to better understand the sentiment of brands like yours. Or the pricing team, who hired a bunch of data scientists to improve the pricing models and a load of technology to help. How about the IT department, who have created a team of developers to build applications and dabble with that endless data warehouse project but for some reason just don't get data?

You are already 'doing data'. Guaranteed. It's just that at this stage it's likely to be a bit of a mess. No coordination. No direction. Huge duplication. Data empires being built all over the place. The wrong skills doing the wrong jobs. Inefficient technology procurement and multiple tools doing the same task. A perception (or reality) that the quality of data is terrible and no data management in place to assure it. No one knows who owns the data. Multiple definitions of sales and 30% of every management meeting spent discussing which sales figure is correct. Does any of this sound familiar? In many organisations this will be a common story.

The challenge this creates

This all presents a problem. A few problems, actually.

Have you heard the phrase 'crap in, crap out'? This has been around for a long time. A more up-to-date version would be 'crap data plus AI equals crap AI'. It's the premise that if you put poor-quality data into a system, then anything you do with it will be equally poor or even worse. Poor-quality data infests your core applications (CRM, enterprise resource planning (ERP), human resources (HR) system etc) and ends up in reports and AI, resulting in misleading charts and potentially dangerous AI models.

This in turn creates problems in making good decisions and being able to take action based on those decisions, without which you may as well pack up and go home. This makes the starting point particularly challenging and, unlike a start-up, you may have legacy data and technology to deal with and history to untangle.

Often a more challenging problem this creates is in the day-to-day operational management of the business. Many business problems that organisations see are rooted in data problems. For example, customers receiving more items than they ordered, orders being made against products that are no longer stocked, suppliers being paid late as invoice dates are incorrect, high cost of machinery fixes because servicing dates are wrong in the system, missed payments as statuses are not updated correctly – all these challenges come from poor management of data. They can cause cash flow issues, brand damage, customer complaints, increased cost and misdirected efforts internally.

Finally, and this impacts most organisations to some degree, there's regulation. Regulation at its highest level is about rules and guidelines designed to make sure that individuals, businesses and organisations operate in a fair, safe and ethical way to protect public interests, promote stability and build trust. This often becomes a data-related challenge because enforcing rules requires accurate, secure and transparent management of data, whether that's tracking financial transactions, ensuring product safety or protecting personal information.

What you should do about it

What you need to help solve all of these challenges is strong data management. This should be about making it easier and simpler for individuals and organisations to a) appropriately access and benefit from fit-for-purpose data as the basis of decision making, b) conduct business simply, effectively and efficiently and c) meet regulatory obligations.

At this stage of the Level Up Framework, it's about clarifying that data management is a requirement, the problems it solves, the benefits it enables and the impact of not investing in it. It's vital that data management isn't seen as a separate activity, independent of running the business or delivering value, but rather as connected and aligned to the data and AI objectives. It's also vital that any specific project or initiative to improve the management of data is clearly understood and aligned to the strategic and operational objectives within the organisation.

For example, acquiring more customers requires us to understand who our customers are, what they look like, how they behave. This has a case in its own right – more customers generate more income – so now we have line of sight between investing in the creation of consistent quality centralised customer data and some critical business value.

Educate and tell stories

Most people 'get' that data has an important part to play in business. Increasingly, as the dust settles on the hype, people are starting to 'get' how AI has an equally important part to play in the current operations and shaping the future business. What's less common is a clear understanding of how it can impact an organisation, in a way that people can really buy into.

At the top level you need to paint a picture about where this can all go. How your industry currently is and could be impacted by data and AI. Think about the legal sector and the impact automated decisions could have on judges and lawyers. How about farmers and the way they assess crops, their quality, the soil composition? The music, film and entertainment industries, the way people consume content and the role AI can play in the creation and serving of that content. With GenAI, we can now do things in these more creative industries using technology than we could ever do before, speeding up production and democratising skills. Generating images, movies, stories, all at the click of a button.

It's important that your organisation can make an informed decision on whether you lead the way, follow others or ignore it completely, although we don't recommend the third option. You need to show the art of the possible. Have you taken your leadership team and key stakeholders to the market-leading players or data and digital native organisations to see how they use data and AI to potent effect? If you're in the public sector and engaging with citizens, have you talked to retailers and brands about how they use data to better understand customer behaviour to drive engagement? How about getting the market-leading technology vendors in front of your organisation to share stories from around the world of how AI is being used for commercial, societal and personal benefit?

This all helps to set the scene and build some excitement behind the opportunity, demonstrate what good looks like and deliberately build towards that.

It is equally important to establish specific opportunities within your business, how data can play a part and the impact it can have. You must communicate clearly how this all enables your business objectives. Vision is great, but unless people can touch and feel what it means to them today, tomorrow and down the line, it can feel out of reach for your business and demotivate rather than inspire. This should form part of an overarching strategy for how you will achieve those business opportunities.

Build out your strategy

Your strategy should act as a framework that describes how you will deliver business value through the application of data and analytics. We discuss our six-pillar approach to defining a data strategy in Part 4; however, we have summarised the main focus areas for the pillars here.

Your strategy should set a north star for your business. A place that you are aiming to get to. A vision that describes in a sentence or two why you are doing what you are doing. It should help to articulate, in plain language, the purpose behind what you will do. What would this be for your organisation?

How about using data to transform the lives of your customers? What about sharing insights with your business partners to build strong, long-lasting relationships? Or what about improving decision making so that products and services best match the demands of your citizens?

Your strategy should also articulate which parts of your business data will be focused on supporting. Ideally, this is based on work you've done to understand the business capabilities in the organisation and those that need remediation, and that remediation is based on the business's strategic objectives.

This is critical. Your strategy is about identifying the parts of your business data that can be used to improve. It's a business strategy and should first and foremost talk about business outcomes and the capabilities needed to operationalise your outcomes. You should be looking to identify business problems or opportunities to focus on, along with the size of the prize.

For example, this could be about increasing customer acquisition, removing blockers in business processes or improving pricing for your products or services. It could be putting a price tag on your data for external monetisation. It could be about reducing the cost of running the business or, in regulated businesses, ensuring you're compliant. These use cases are the pots of gold that form the basis of your investment case and are key to establishing your agenda.

Data evangelist Pete Williams says:

> 'Every business is driven by a commercial strategy. Even a "data" business is selling the data it generates. So your data strategy must be an informer and an enabler of the business outcomes. As such it must be closely tied to the success factors of each of the C suite responsibilities for them to care. The challenge is getting to speak to them often and in enough detail to help them to understand and want to sponsor your ideas. A tech focused data strategy will exist in a fragile bubble that will burst as soon as times are challenging. A commercially focused data strategy forms an effective shelter to help survive the bad times but take advantage of the good when they come.'[24]

The vision and these use cases are top priority. The rest of your strategy and approach hang off these and ensure you are focused on adding incremental value to the organisation.

To define what changes you need to make that will allow you to deliver those use cases, you will need to understand your existing capabilities and how much value is currently being delivered from data. How much AI is playing a part today, if at all. This means

---

24 Interview with Pete Williams, 20 November 2024

looking at your team, skills, the organisational structure, how you work, the technologies in place and how well they are set up, the way you manage and govern data and how culturally aligned the mindset of your business is to make best use of data and new technologies. It's good to see how you stack up against others in your industry that you consider your competition so you have a benchmark. Naturally, blockers will pop out during an assessment like this, but be careful not to make too many assumptions about what is and isn't possible.

Technology is a fundamental enabler for success with data, so gain a clear understanding of the organisation's general technology strategy and what decisions have already been made about data, analytics and AI tools. The guidelines, no-go areas and key principles of the technology strategy and main gaps to plug are important to get clear. You'll use this to inform some of the bigger investments required. However, as you will see in the next stage, we don't believe it's right to run into big technology investments until you have proved you can deliver incremental business value.

With the direction set and a clear understanding of the capability gaps that exist, you need to define your roadmap for how you will deliver business value and build the necessary capabilities in the coming months and years. The Level Up Framework gives you a structure for this roadmap.

Your strategy should be used as a communication tool – a narrative to explain where you are heading and how you will get there. It's not a bible, but a roadmap that steers your journey, gets adjusted as required and against which progress is measured.

Understand stakeholder buy-in

Data shouldn't be in a silo. Business value from data and AI will almost certainly not be limited to one team, one business problem or one area of your organisation. Data (and its value) is pervasive and prevalent in every customer interaction, every system key stroke, every employee connection. As the world becomes more digital and more AI enabled, this paradigm is increasingly important.

The opportunity that exists can be applied to most parts of your business. Nearly all the people in your organisation are your stakeholders. This is a unique challenge for data strategies. Possibly the only other areas in the business like that are HR and finance, with which everyone will have need to have some interaction.

Stakeholder engagement and more importantly buy-in are critical to your success overall but particularly at these burgeoning stages of the journey. At a minimum you will need to understand the relative buy-in of the key budget-holders, decision-makers and influencers in the organisation.

Buy-in can be understood from two angles: (1) clarity and understanding of the business outcome and (2) experience and evidence of the outcome that data and AI can give to that individual or the organisation as a whole. The matrix below is a way to plot buy-in of the key stakeholders and then put in appropriate interventions that ensure you have the right commitment from the right people.

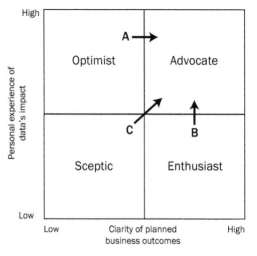

Stakeholder buy-in matrix

This produces four types of people associated with their level of buy-in:

- **The optimist:** they have seen data and/or AI add value before so they get it and are up for it but don't yet know what value it will add to this company.

- **The enthusiast:** they understand what value data and/or AI can add to the company and are keen to make it happen but they have no personal experience of it working. We could call them cautious optimists.

- **The sceptic:** they have never seen data and/or AI work for a business and don't get how it can for your business. These are clearly the least bought in.

- **The advocate:** they have seen it work before, understand how it can add value to your business and have properly bought into what you are trying to achieve.

A different approach will be needed for each of these groups and you should ensure you have enough advocates to help punch through to the next stage.

At a workshop we ran recently with the leadership team of a retailer, we asked for examples of where they had worked at other companies that had created strategic benefit from data and AI. We heard examples from travel platform booking.com, retailer ASOS, Lego, supermarket chain Tesco, optometrist Spec-savers and others. The people in the room had experience of this being successful in the past.

We later asked about their understanding and perceptions of outcomes and feasibility within their organisation. There was great understanding of what problems to solve, but less confidence on the ability to achieve a solution based on the feasibility. This gave us a clear indication of what was required for this leadership team to create better buy-in.

Create a starter team

You will need to build your minimum efficient organisation. That is, the leanest team possible to ensure you can effectively get through this stage and be prepared to move at pace through the next stage, Prove Value.

This stage and team are best led by someone with relative seniority within the organisation. Someone who can own the definition and execution of a business-focused strategy. Someone who can engage and influence people across the business and position effectively to the board and senior leadership team. The CDO is a role that could take this responsibility and has grown in importance in recent years as companies try to get a handle on their data strategy. We explore the role of the CDO further in Part 4.

Those without a CDO will still need to ensure they have someone in the organisation able to set and lead the strategy. Without this capability, it is tough to get any traction.

AI raises some other questions about where this is best led from. Since AI is as much about digital, technology, process re-engineering, system integration, innovation and business change as it is about data, there are options for which person or department is most appropriate in your organisation. People from data, digital, transformation, technology, research and development (R&D), operations, the CEO – they could all be candidates to own and lead this. As could your CDO.

The decision on where the role lands is important, but not as important as actually making the decision. No stated owner (or owners) will only lead to proliferation, risk, inefficiencies and potentially regretted investments.

Regardless of who takes that leadership responsibility, they will want to build a team with the energy, focus and passion to truly understand and care for the business outcomes and a culture of developing high-performing, innovative and agile teams. A crack team that can roll up their sleeves and get things done. You'll want to start small and grow out from this team so they will set the tone for how your focused people operate. Regardless of what level your organisation is at, this strategy needs leadership at a top level to get traction and momentum. Change needs leadership.

Since part of the point of this stage is to define future roles, responsibilities and organisational structure, to some degree where this team sits is not important. What is important is that they are given autonomy and support to help shape the agenda and break down silos.

Initiating culture change

In Part 1 we talked about the importance of having a data-guided culture that's embedded into the beliefs, values and attitudes of your business. A culture where decisions are made by marrying data with experience and intuition. A culture where AI is understood for what it is and what it can provide, and used where it is most valuable. A culture where change and being adaptable are assumed and embraced. We also explained how if you want to embrace AI or improve your use of data, you will need to change your culture in some way.

At this stage of the journey, while you're establishing the agenda, initiating that culture change should be focused around engagement and education. Engage the people in your organisation so they feel connected and consulted, and educate them so they aren't in the dark and have the knowledge they need to contribute to the change.

The success of any attempts at culture shift requires collaboration and strong relationships. This is underpinned by using communication as an agent for change. Strong, regular and clear communication at this stage is a sure-fire way to get off the ground and set yourself up for success.

Using everything you have learned in this chapter on education, defining a strategy, engaging stakeholders, getting your team together and building and sharing your pitch deck (covered in the next part of this section) requires some epic communication skills. At this point, and throughout this journey, it's important to remember that people engage with messages in different ways. You need to consider the format and approach you use depending on the audience, the message and the communication channel.

The twenty-slide PowerPoint presentation used in a meeting may not land well with everyone if it's sent via email or stored on your intranet. Some people will want to feel like they are getting formal training on a course, while others will respond to a workshop or engagement session. The important thing is that you are using communication to tell stories, explain concepts, take input, get a feel for organisational readiness and raise the IQ of the organisation.

To do that, think about the lens you put on what you are communicating. The chief finance officer (CFO) will need a different lens on the strategy to the chief technology officer (CTO), and they will both need a different lens to an analytics team or the line of department leads. One size doesn't fit all and tailoring the approach, personalising the message and targeting your communication will help to ensure you establish a strong agenda.

Giving people options for how they consume content helps maximise engagement and increases the chances of your message landing and being understood. Get creative. Use videos, blogs, demonstrations, newsletters, articles, animations, show and tells, question and answer and 'ask me anything' sessions. This is about communicating your message, building credibility, establishing a culture of sharing and collaboration, getting buy-in and ensuring your strategy is clear and understood.

This is also the time to learn the actual culture of the organisation as it relates to data and AI, determine where you need to be, and define a plan for how you will re-anchor the business around the cultural norms required to meet the potential opportunity that data and AI provide.

Finally, we cannot overstate enough the importance of this change and culture being championed and led by senior leadership. In most organisations where hierarchy exists, there is a conscious or unconscious bias towards following the lead shown by those at more senior levels. If they aren't on board, aren't championing, aren't demonstrating the behaviours that the change requires, then typically the organisation won't follow.

Change isn't only top down like this. In fact, it's critical for bottom-up change to happen, but progress will be hampered without the correct behaviours shown at the very top.

Build the case and get investment

You need to know how big an impact you can make on your organisation and where that impact could be felt. Is this a £1, £1 million or £100 million opportunity? Have you worked out which elements of the business strategy you can impact and at what scale?

Hidden within your organisation are pots of gold that can help improve your key business metrics. By applying data-guided thinking, there will be opportunities to increase your revenues, reduce the cost of your operations, build stronger relationships with partners and suppliers, understand and engage your employees and customers, build better products and enter new markets.

Knowing the size of the prize is critical. Once we know, we need to be able to articulate this alongside the investment required. Many data initiatives are focused on developing data capabilities within the organisation (like data governance, building technology platforms, recruiting data scientists) and not on delivering incremental value. The size of the prize is often a forgotten piece when asking for investment.

Budget may still get allocated this way but this will undoubtedly cause issues further along the journey when money has been invested and no return has been felt.

Your organisation will have its own internal process for approving expenditure, deciding whether that spend is operating expenditure (OPEX) or capital expenditure (CAPEX), budget cycles, investment proposals, return on investment (ROI) or internal rate of return (IRR) hurdles to hit. You should lay some groundwork ahead of those formal discussions by telling the story in a way that effectively conveys your message about your case and investment requirements.

This is a sales pitch. You are trying to get your organisation behind the outcome you are confident you can achieve, sell those benefits and make it clear you have a well thought out plan to move the agenda forward. You should think about this like a start-up goes about getting angel, seed or series funding. You need a pitch deck and you should spend time looking at formulas that work for getting your pitch right. The table below shows headings and descriptions that you should consider including in your budget request presentation.

| *Vision* | This is a one-sentence overview of what you are looking to achieve and the value you expect to bring to the organisation. It's your 'elevator' pitch. Keep it short, simple and jargon-free. This is your why, your purpose for doing this. |

Business opportunity	Use this slide to articulate the total size of the opportunity. Be as broad as possible but frame it in terms of the business strategy and try to break it down into areas of the business you can address with data. Be clear on what return is available. This is you focusing on what you can genuinely achieve.
The problem	Use this section to summarise why the organisation struggles to reach this business opportunity. What's stopping you from achieving the prize now? Try to tell a relatable story about the challenges to make the problem as real as possible and how it impacts your goals. Don't get too far into the weeds.
The solution	Now you can start talking about the how. You will be tempted to put this earlier in the presentation but resist that. You get to dive into describing the capabilities you will need to put in place across the business. You are describing how the solution helps remove problems to achieve the business opportunity.
Roadmap	You should use this section to show, ideally on a single page, your plan for achieving the solution and therefore the business opportunities. Be pragmatic and realistic about this and have your assumptions ready so you can explain how the plan is made up.

Investment needs	You're now in a position to explain your investment requirements. You will want to explain how much you think you will need across your planning horizon, how much you need to get through the next stage of the Level Up Framework (Prove Value), how you will be spending the money and how it contributes to the goals.

Establish the Agenda: The breakthrough criteria

There are a number of must-have outcomes you need to have reached by the end of this stage. These outcomes give you what you need in order to punch through to the next stage and ensure strong foundations are in place.

1. **Organisational buy-in:** at this stage you are looking for enough buy-in from the organisation to ensure you have people who are interested and rooting for success. We're talking emotional buy-in – some top down, some bottom up.

2. **Strategic backing:** success with data and AI needs to be of strategic importance, aligned to the business goals and of significance to the success of the organisation.

3. **Pots of gold identified:** you need to know where the best opportunities or challenges are, what

the size of the prize is and what the relative priorities are.

4. **Minimum efficient organisation in place:** the right team ready to deliver the Prove Value stage.

5. **Pitch deck:** bringing together the vision, strategy, pots of gold and investments required into a solid story, tailored to the audience with the right lens.

6. **Investment required:** you will have assessed the costs necessary to deliver the strategy and a roadmap of investments you are likely to make along the way.

7. **Plan for the Prove Value stage:** a clear plan for the next stage of the journey. What will you do next?

8. **Funding for the Prove Value stage:** you'll want enough funding to prove value, refine your plan and start building capability.

THREE

Prove Value

In October 2007, Brian Chesky and his roommate Joe Gebbia were unemployed and looking for a way to make some extra cash to pay rent. There was a major shortage of hotel rooms and traditional accommodation in San Francisco as there were several conferences coming up.

Chesky and Gebbia decided to rent out part of their apartment to people struggling to find somewhere to stay. They put together a basic website called airbedandbreakfast.com, which offered an airbed in their loft and a homemade breakfast the following morning for $80 per night.

Over the next eleven years and after some early failed attempts to scale the business, get the proposition right and secure investment, Airbnb scaled to a $31 billion valuation and secured $4.4 billion investment. It is a global phenomenon.

Three people showed up in October 2007, which proved to the founders that they had a proposition. No big investment. No extensive business case. No investment in a huge team to start the idea. No major technology platform. Just a concept that needed testing and proof that they could get value from something.

According to Chesky, 'People have said that [Airbnb is] the worst idea that ever worked.'[25]

They proved that there was a demand for what seemed at the time like a crazy idea. On the face of it, letting a stranger into your house to stay overnight sounded like a ridiculous idea. Who would want to offer that? Who would want to stay?

Airbnb and many other start-ups like it have shown us that it's worth proving value before starting to scale, get or make big investments. Until the founders landed on the right business model that worked, proved successful and showed that the idea was credible, they couldn't take it forward, big or fast. Getting data right needs this same mentality and approach.

---

25 C Garing, 'Airbnb founder: Company "wasn't supposed to be the big idea"', *Vanity Fair* (9 October 2014), www.vanityfair.com/news/tech/2014/10/airbnb-founder-big-idea-logo, accessed 10 January 2025

Gaining credibility

The hard work during Establish the Agenda was all about getting clarity on the potential opportunity for your organisation, understanding how well set up the business is to achieve that opportunity and creating an agile and iterative plan.

Armed with your initial funding, this next step is to do what Chesky and Gebbia did and prove value. Before pushing hard on further deep investments, it's vital that you gain credibility by demonstrating that applying data to known and necessary business challenges can add value to the business.

If your aim is to create a business guided by data, the journey you go on should apply that concept. Use evidence that proves as an organisation you can make this work before you decide to press on. While you want to aim for the best possible return, it's likely that you'll make small gains and small returns compared to what was previously defined as the size of the prize. This is fine and expected. It's what you want, really – small investment, prove you can get a return and create some data points of success.

During this stage you'll be looking to further validate your assumptions on your strategy and pivot accordingly. As you learn and start this process there will be blockers, changes and recruitment challenges so we need to keep an eye on the next move and not be afraid to change our approach.

What's important is the business outcome. The route will change and your plans will change. Openness and honesty, coupled with positive delivery, help to build credibility and trust that you know what you are doing and why. Working alongside and in collaboration with your peers and colleagues at this stage will not only help gain credibility but also build relationships and pave the way for easier and sharper communication when things change or don't go to plan.

New concepts need a new mindset

The concept of proving value, starting small and then scaling is alien to many, particularly when it comes to securing budget, so this stage should aim to embed this mindset into the organisation. There will be many new ways of working for technology teams, for data teams, for how commercial teams engage and this is the stage where you can start to embed a new cultural mindset.

This is the mindset we want you to have during this whole journey, not just at this stage. Start small, prove value, then scale, accelerate and optimise. Prove first then take an idea forward, whether you are building a dashboard, launching a data product, taking a new proposition to market, or building a data flow or new algorithm. It's the best way to prove that something is heading in the right direction and worth investing in before jumping in and increasing spend.

This is likely for many to be a cultural adjustment, but ultimately you build the right thing faster, rather than taking a long time to build something big that was never going to work in the first place. It's a cultural adjustment worth making.

Build and activate a data product

The problem with the way organisations have traditionally tried to get off the ground with data strategies is that they focus on building perfect solutions from the start with no clear set of business use cases. They get investment to build a company-wide data warehouse and start bringing data together, building data models and dashboards based on user requirements. The challenge here is that there is no link to the changes the business will make or the outcomes they're looking to achieve. It's more like a technology platform with no purpose, rather than a business solution with real impact.

Packaging up a business outcome, the technology and the data required to support that outcome means we need to start thinking about the planning and execution of solutions through a product development lens and moving from data solutions to data products.

This product-centric approach allows you to scale individual and isolated successes into sustainable, organisation-wide, data-guided decisions that need to be the foundation of your data strategy.

We discuss the product development approach and roles required elsewhere in this book but for now the important part is that this stage of the journey requires you to prove value and credibility by identifying a challenge or problem, developing a solution and taking steps to achieve some of the business value associated with it. A mechanism that allows for rapid iteration and adjustments that mean you can change the solution as you learn how it impacts the business.

You should pick one of the use cases identified at the Establish stage (for example: improve customer retention, increase open rates on emails, reduce the time to carry out a process) and one that can be developed at low cost to quickly determine whether you can achieve the improvements you believed were possible. This is about proving to yourself, your business and your stakeholders that by applying data to a decision and therefore a business outcome, you can make some improvements, or at the very least learn that you can't.

When you pick a use case, it's important to think about the end outcome you are trying to impact. The data product doesn't stop at the development of a solution but at the implementation of a change that impacts the end customer, stakeholder or process. Consider a few use cases to decide which you think is the most feasible because of access to the data, the technology and the skills required, balanced against the value that is potentially achievable.

We can use the business capability map discussed earlier for this, so let's look at a quick example to bring it to life. Your CEO has determined that the manufacturing of products is too slow, so you speak to the head of operations and review the business capabilities around supply chain. The objective here is to identify which business capability, or capabilities, is causing you the problem and slowing down production to help you understand what needs to happen for the production process to work more smoothly, ie all outputs are available at the right time and in the right quantity. You can then identify where the root cause is by assessing each part of that business capability. For example, you may identify that it's the sourcing of raw materials that is slowing you down.

Often your organisation has the information needed for this work, but the data is in different systems, the systems' inputs don't align, the processes are working against each other, and no one understands how their input affects other parts of the process. This gives you a great use case at this stage – sort the data and fix the problem, a compelling set of objectives.

From here, you should be looking to build a starter data product to meet these objectives. Not one with all the bells and whistles but an MVP or solution that brings together the data, builds a basic data model and delivers insight that can be acted upon. Being acted upon is the vital component to validate that you have been able to move a needle and get some of the business value associated with the use case.

Think of what you are building here as a prototype or a test. A test for new ways of working. A test that you can treat data as a product. A test of bringing people together and collaborating in ways they may have not before. A test of achieving improvements to your chosen use case. These factors come together to try to achieve a result and in the process prove value and gain credibility.

The aims of this initial data product build are that you impact your business outcomes in some way, learn from it and can demonstrate and communicate all this to the business stakeholders. You will use this MVP and others like it as a basis for growth in the next stages of the framework.

This idea of building an MVP or starter data product is summarised nicely by Jagpal Jheeta, a business and technology director with experience across organisations such as Marks & Spencer, Symphony EYC, Royal Mail and the Financial Conduct Authority:

'In business, as in life, we make progress by connecting and collaborating, bringing together the best ideas from our networks, testing, scaling and industrialising as fast as possible. AI in all its forms will enable us to do this faster, and so we need the right data in the right place at the right time. We need to be selective and laser focused on initiatives that can move the dial, while understanding and stopping those that don't. Building, testing, deploying and continuously iterating faster and faster will be how organisations win. Recognising that tomorrow's data needs will be different to the data needs of today will set organisations up for success.'[26]

Rapid provision of insights

During these early stages of your journey, you are likely to come up against resistance to anything new around analytics, algorithms, the potential of AI and exciting use cases if your stakeholders are unable to get reports that tell them how the company performed last week. For all the exciting benefits that you know are waiting to be unlocked, there is no getting away from the fact that everyone will want access to reports and dashboards that give them better clarity over the key metrics of the organisation.

Visibility of metrics is vital to an organisation's ability to understand where it has come from, know how it is performing today and see indications of what may be

---

26 Interview with Jagpal Jheeta, 10 November 2024

coming down the line. This is the lifeblood of a leader-ship team's ability to understand whether the actions and strategies they have in place are impacting the outcomes. There will always be a thirst for these macro-level insights. At this stage of the journey, when you should be looking to prove value and build cred-ibility, it is sensible to allocate some focus to rapidly providing data products that support this thirst.

There are several issues to watch out for:

1. Reports add limited value if they aren't aligned to key outcomes.

2. People often don't know what they need until they see it so it's possible that you could spend hours building reports and dashboards that never get used.

3. Unless you have actively ensured that metric definitions are agreed, you can end up creating more problems than you solve.

4. It can be hard to prioritise where to invest time and which metrics to build.

5. It can be challenging to deliver clean, accurate metrics as the underlying data work required has yet to be carried out.

All of these 'watch outs' can lead to big investments in 'sorting out core reporting' with limited value or overall benefit to the agenda.

What's needed is the rapid provision of insights that prioritise the most impactful metrics and deliver those as data products to the stakeholders who have the biggest influence over the performance of that metric. Even though the objective is to deliver insights, you are still looking to focus on the things that could have the biggest impact on the outcomes of the business. Focus on the outcomes and actions you want to drive rather than the report/dashboard itself. The destination is the change and not the data product (dashboard) itself.

The other valuable step that can be taken is to unlock data access to the analysts or data scientists in the organisation so they can gain insights themselves. There is often a concern about this as it may mean you are creating duplication of effort or new cottage industries. But with good governance this can be a valuable way to accelerate getting data in the hands of the right people and not creating new blockers.

Putting in place foundational capabilities

While the priority for this stage is to prove value by getting hands dirty and building data products focused on business outcomes, it's also the time to start building the capabilities that will form the basis of your data strategy. Capabilities should be built relative to where you are in the journey and the level of incremental business value that you have delivered at that stage.

You aren't yet ready to swamp the organisation with new technology, teams of data scientists, data engineers or other roles as you are still in the process of proving value. What's needed is a next iteration of growing out your capabilities – a first fix. Remember we talked about getting seed funding as part of the Establish stage? Along with the investment in some early data products, these capabilities are what you want to invest in further during this stage.

The key foundational capabilities to consider at this stage of your journey cover:

1. Building your minimum efficient organisation

2. Initiating your new approach and ceremonies

3. Putting in place starter technology and architecture that can scale

4. Creating momentum on resolving core data issues

5. Using communication as a change agent

Building your minimum efficient organisation

You need to enhance your team so that you can deliver this stage but also be ready to move into the Scale phase of the Level Up Framework. This will build on the starter team put in place during Establish, and the mix implemented there will change what you look to bring together here. You want to be building your 'minimum efficient organisation' at this stage – the smallest team required to build and activate the data product and rapid insights mentioned earlier.

Consider the following groups of skills that will form the basis of what's needed to build those data products and further prepare the organisation. Note that these are groups of discipline rather than names of roles.

Business discovery

Having a team that's able to engage with the broader business to understand how it operates – the processes, the key metrics, what's important to the leaders and front-line staff – is critical to delivering outcomes and data products that have impact.

The disciplines required are as follows:

- **Product management** is the practice of strategically driving the development, launch and continual support and improvement of your organisation's data products.

- **Business analysis** enables change by understanding problems and opportunities, defining needs and recommending solutions that deliver value. They are agents of change.

- **Business enablement** works to ensure that the organisation is ready, educated and able to understand data in a way that helps them make decisions, implement change and create action.

Delivery

Visions or strategies without a plan are just ideas and aspirations, and a plan without action is just a nice Gantt chart, product backlog or Kanban board. The delivery discipline comprises the skills required to get the development of data products and technology solutions planned, designed, built and delivered.

- **Architecture and design** make up the practice of strategically defining the technology, tools, underlying architecture and design required to deliver the organisation's data products.

- **Engineering** is the craft that develops and tests the solution underpinning the data products, including building data pipelines and structured data sets.

- **Data science** allows rules, mathematical models and scientific methods to be applied to data to identify patterns and insights, and builds models to feed your data products.

- **Analytics and business intelligence** help to answer business questions by visualising data and solving business problems.

Data management

We have previously discussed the need for data management and the foundation this provides for understanding, managing and building confidence and transparency in the data you have. This transparency and understanding help an organisation to interact effectively with its people, products, customers, operations and money. This discipline helps to ensure the delivery of trustworthy data for the business, ready to be harnessed to generate value. We do this by building connections, as we capture and understand the organisation's ecosystem.

- **Assurance** is the practice of defining and implementing steps to assure data in terms of its quality, consistency, accuracy, timeliness and accessibility through the end-to-end data value chain.

- **Protection** is the practice of putting in place controls to protect an organisation's data assets in terms of physical and cyber security controls.

- **Adherence** is the work required to ensure the process of assurance and protection is adhered to.

You may be bringing people in from outside your organisation, either through recruitment, contracting or consultancy. You may be consolidating from across your organisation or you may be cross-training people to carry out these functions. The decision here will depend on the preferred approach, pace of change you'd like to move at or what you are used to.

One example of this type of organisation was developed by Ryan den Rooijen, when he was the CDO of Chalhoub Group, the leading luxury retailer in the Middle East. Ryan stated:

> 'When I started in my role I was keen to hit the ground running. Therefore, instead of building a lot of siloed teams centred around capabilities, eg data engineering, data science, etc. I instead established three pillars focused on outcomes: assets, products and impact.
>
> 'Data assets are tasked with ensuring data quality, architecture and management.
>
> 'Data products identifies opportunities for products and then delivers them end to end.
>
> 'Analytics impact focuses on delivering operational transformation and profitability.
>
> 'This model's emphasis on outputs enabled us to quickly deliver business value, while simplifying stakeholder communications. Everyone could understand what the team did.
>
> 'Additionally, by recruiting "bottom up" we were able to demonstrate progress every step of the way as we grew the team, instead of waiting for our leadership to be recruited before starting.

'Finally, where historically these functions would have existed within the data team, increasingly there is sense and discussion about these pillars being embedded across data, technology and business teams.'[27]

Initiating your new approach and ceremonies

The way you operate and your approach to planning and tracking progress establish early on that you will be focused on: i) action, ii) scaling out the people involved, and iii) the commitments being made.

To be adaptable and agile, a step change is often required in the approach used to deliver your data strategy. At this early stage it is important to establish this change and set clear team values, culture and behaviours that allow you to work at pace, engage well with the wider business organisation and focus on business outcomes, not just data and technology.

From an objective planning perspective, this means taking the strategy and breaking that down into an overarching one-year goal (for example, deliver £1 million of business benefit, gain ISO accreditation, sell our data to three of our external stakeholders), then into quarterly outcomes and key results (OKRs), monthly team plans and fortnightly sprints. Maintaining a backlog that is open and shared across the

---

27 Interview with Ryan den Rooijen, 7 January 2024

team means you remain focused on the outcomes that align back to the one-year goal and ultimately the business strategy.

We have defined the key concepts and definitions to be used as part of this approach, which prioritises outcomes, communication, collaboration and getting work done over micromanagement, big up-front planning and working in silos. These are as follows:

- **Backlog:** the list of everything that is needed or has been requested that could add value.

- **Backlog refinement:** the practice of improving user stories, acceptance criteria, test cases and other information that is relevant to each backlog item, providing sufficient detail and confidence for the business stakeholder to make informed decisions on the priorities for the next sprint.

- **Business stakeholder:** the person delegated from a business team to work closely with the data team as part of the development process, and responsible for prioritisation. This should be a member of the business unit's leadership team who has a strong commercial understanding and can be trusted to fairly represent interests across the business unit.

- **Daily stand-up:** the daily meeting with everyone associated with the sprint goals. Occurring at the same time each day, it runs for fifteen minutes and takes place regardless of absences. People report what they completed the previous day, what they are working on today and any blockers. New issues are captured. Colleagues can call out areas where help or collaboration are required. This is intended as a quick summary for the team only; it is not a meeting to define solutions or a stakeholder actions meeting.

- **Epic:** a lengthy user story that cannot be completed in one sprint.

- **Show and tell:** a meeting facilitated by the product owner that is used to demonstrate the work completed during the sprint. Business stakeholders and/or end users may attend. Those in attendance agree what has been completed (and what hasn't) so that this can be released to the business.

- **Sprint:** the two-week-long development process during which the team completes tasks to deliver stories and epics.

- **Sprint planning:** a meeting attended by the product owner and the business team. Outside stakeholders may attend as needed. The product owner describes the highest priority features to the team.

- **Sprint retrospective:** a meeting facilitated by the product owner to discuss the sprint and determine what could be changed to make the next sprint more productive.

- **Steering group:** a group of stakeholders who decide on the priority and order of process for the project or workflow programmes that the organisation is delivering. This should consist of some or all of the leadership team for the business unit and could take place as a standing agenda item at a monthly leadership team meeting.

- **Task:** the discrete pieces of work that are required to deliver a story.

- **Theme:** a group of user stories that share a common business goal or objective. For example, if the business objective was to improve customer satisfaction, all the reporting created to support that initiative would be grouped under that theme.

- **User story:** short requirements written from the perspective of an end user. They take the form of: 'As an X, I would like to have Y so that I can do Z.'

- **Workstream alignment:** a monthly meeting of all the data product owners. It is an opportunity for each product owner to provide an update from their area, discuss future work and dependencies and get aligned across the group.

You should also look to establish KPIs for the team and data strategy to benchmark and track progress. This keeps you honest and ensures that everyone is aware of the impact they individually have on the outcomes and how collectively you are impacting on the organisation. We cover this in more detail in Part 4.

Putting in place starter technology
and architecture that can scale

There can be a temptation to prioritise buying or sorting technology ahead of anything else but there are several things to get right and to put in place before this stage. You may have some data technology already or an existing/legacy technology estate in place. This is either a great thing as you have the technology you need or it is holding you back, depending on the previous choices made. You may be starting from scratch and have little or nothing in place, in which case the technology market will be a daunting place to go fishing in.

Either way, we need to ensure that what we put in place is exactly what is required to move you through the Prove Value stage but has the ability to grow with you into the Scale stage and beyond. You don't need a gold-plated solution that is able to satisfy every requirement you can think of for capabilities needed at the Accelerate or Optimise stages of the Level Up Framework. If you do that you will be investing in technology that you won't be able to maximise, leading to wasted investment.

You need a starter technology platform that is small, lightweight, low cost and adaptable, with only the components necessary to build and activate your initial data product and to build the rapid insights identified as priority. The aim here is to prove that you can move the needle – not take over the world. Cloud technology has been a key enabler to this approach and should form a key part of your thinking if you want agility and flexibility. Cloud provides the ability to scale up and down as demand changes and enables a smaller investment to get started that can grow and scale as you grow and scale.

The importance of use cases

In designing and building your adaptable data platform, use cases matter. They matter for many reasons but there are three which are key: (1) picking the right technology, (2) helping with prioritisation, and (3) helping make design decisions.

Firstly, without understanding your use cases you can't pick the right technology. If, for example, you don't understand that your marketing team wants to make real-time product recommendations to customers browsing your website, based on their page views, previous purchases and visit history, there is no way you can establish the kind of data platform and infrastructure to support that requirement. That's different from just looking to build some solid business intelligence and reporting capability, for which the architecture and design decisions would be very different.

Secondly, the prioritisation of your use cases makes a huge difference to the order in which you should buy technology and build the architecture. In what order are you going to tackle building your platform? That needs to be aligned to the use cases that are important and the order in which you will deliver them. You will have a vision for what your data platform can achieve but it's unlikely you will need everything on day one. Tie your early decisions about technology and what you implement back to your use cases, identify the most value-driving themes and do those first. This also helps you to unpick the technology market and know which tools you should and shouldn't consider. It can be easy to fall for the sales pitch of the data vendors without properly understanding what you are looking for, why and when. Having that clarity of use case and therefore the functionality you need will help to better articulate need, shortlist technology candidates and make a sensible selection.

Thirdly, all your architectural design decisions are going to come back to the use cases. Choosing technology that can scale, the performance you require from it, the security that you may need in place, the functionality it needs to deliver, the data you need to ingest, the data model you need to build. For all of those decisions you're going to need to refer back to the use cases you're trying to deliver. Without doing this you can end up investing in building a shiny data platform with all the latest functionality and trendiest tech that doesn't meet the needs of the business or, alternatively, a substandard platform that can't deal with the scale, growth or pace of change needed to get the most value from data.

Initiate your starter technology platform

The idea with technology at this stage is to get a starter platform off the ground and set the foundation. This may or may not be technology you already have but the principle of selecting a lightweight, low-additional-cost platform that can be used to prove value and that can scale is paramount. With the growth of the subscription-based model (often called Software as a Service (SaaS)) from technology vendors, it is possible to start small and scale as needed, only consuming and paying for storage and processing that you use, as opposed to paying for the hardware, storage, space on your premises regardless of usage.

This allows you to test the technology on specific use cases and scale when ready. It allows you to get up and running in minutes, rather than weeks or months. This is great as it ensures that initial costs are minimised and only increase when usage (hopefully coupled with value) increases.

During this stage, and to enable you to build your initial data products and rapid insights, you will need to be able to ingest some data sets, for example sales and customer data, store and transform (or model) that data, ensure a level of governance, provide an ability to build dashboards and analyse data and outputs so you can make business decisions. Outcome over perfection is what you are after here and a platform that allows you to do those things will mean you can prove and demonstrate value without investing millions (in implementing new solutions or fixing what you already have) ahead of time.

This won't be your final set-up or platform – you will need to add functionality, add complexity, tighten the governance, allow different workloads to take place – but this is to set you up for success and give you the ammunition required to get investment to start to put more scale and pace through the data products, services and solutions you will want to build next.

The diagram below shows the key capabilities required; the level of complexity your set-up can handle will change, but this is what is required from day one. While there are a number of capabilities, many are consolidated in single platforms provided by major and start-up vendors.

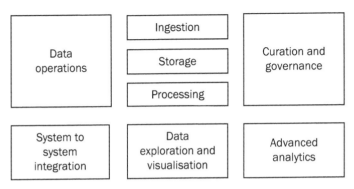

High-level technical capabilities

Your platform should consist of eight high-level conceptual capabilities:

- **Ingestion:** the ability to access, extract and bring together data from various source applications (finance, ERP, CRM, HR, website, supply chain systems, emails, videos, audio files etc) either in regular batch loads of data, near real time in small batches or in real time.

- **Storage:** once you have ingested that data, it will need to be stored in a way that allows it to be accessed when and where required for both operational and innovation purposes. This covers a range of storage mechanisms, different types of data and the ability to archive and share data sets.

- **Process and modelling:** the data you are storing in its raw form will need to be modelled. It will be consolidated, aggregated and improved on by AI models and processing that derive insights, answers to questions and creation of new data and predictions.

- **Curation and governance:** your data assets will need to be organised, enriched and improved through better data quality, management of master and reference data, applying privacy controls and cataloguing your data assets.

- **System to system integration:** this manages the process of taking data from one or more internal or external sources and transporting it to another for storage and/or processing.

- **Data exploration and visualisation:** gaining insights and making decisions is where the value starts to be realised. This component of the platform allows for data to be explored and visualised into reports and dashboards.

- **Advanced analytics and AI:** access to technology and a place for innovation, R&D and advanced modelling elevates capabilities up a level. This provides somewhere to build, train and deploy ML models, and leverage large language models and other GenAI tools.

- **Data operations:** wrapping around all this is the technology needed to securely manage the availability and delivery of data and AI products and services, monitor and control the health of the platforms, manage the infrastructure, plus carry out data and AI lifecycle management and back-up and recovery processes.

These high-level capabilities align closely with the data value chain we looked at earlier. Your data platform is there to move data through the data value chain so that you can reach value realisation.

Creating momentum on resolving core data issues

Earlier, we discussed the need for excellent data management and the importance of the organisation understanding this necessity. As it's not meant to be a separate independent initiative, during this critical Prove Value stage, we've seen it's important to demonstrate the value of resolving core data issues and creating momentum in this area.

For a business-to-consumer entertainment client we worked with, we created a single customer record by pulling together customers from multiple sources, which allowed us to assess their marketing content and present a more accurate record of the addressable customer base than they had before. This showed there were 250,000 more customers opted in to receive marketing communications than they previously thought and had access to – 250,000 more customers to market, promote and sell to.

This was a 100% increase on what they had in their CRM system. They had an average conversion rate of 10% and an average ticket price of £30, which meant they were able to add £750,000 of ticket sales simply by improving the management of their customer data. In fact, by improving the management of one attribute: the opt-in flag of their customers.

At another organisation we worked with, this one in the consumer electronics space, we found that the dimensions of certain products were not being entered in by the product team when they were ranging new products. The products were being created in the system, so orders could be made and shipped to the client's warehouse and their customers, but the dimensions weren't required to make that happen. However, unbeknown to the product team, the dimensions *were* required for the products to be ranged on the website run by the ecommerce team. By not including those dimensions, they were preventing the products from being ranged on the site.

These were previously popular products, so it meant the client organisation was missing out on sales simply because certain attributes hadn't been included against the product during set-up. Resolving this was a simple fix when it became obvious to the product team why it was necessary to add the dimensions.

These are great examples of the kind of work required at the Prove Value stage, and frankly all the time when it comes to managing data better. By finding and closing a data quality gap – aligned to a specific business problem in the case of the consumer electronics client, aligned to a specific business opportunity in the case of the entertainment client – you demonstrate the need and value of strong data management as a discipline.

Using communication as a change agent

During Establish the Agenda, we talked about painting a picture and telling stories. The need for effective communication during this critical Prove Value stage of the journey can't be understated, and it certainly shouldn't be slowed down or restricted. It's the driver of successful culture change. It ensures that people understand the vision, goals and reasons behind the change, and builds a sense of inclusion and shared purpose, rather than change being 'done' to people.

Clear, consistent messaging helps to align individual behaviours with the new cultural norms you're trying to embed, which in turn reduces resistance and builds trust. It encourages feedback and dialogue, meaning you can identify and resolve issues that arise during the transition.

Given all that, how do you get your communication to stick?

Repetition is an extremely effective communication strategy. In marketing and advertising it's been proven that consistent messaging over a sustained period to a specific (or target) audience is necessary to build understanding, trust and acceptance of the message and the brand. The 'rule of seven' suggests that consumers need to hear or see a message seven times before they are likely to take action.[28]

That's a lot of communication to land a message. While the Establish the Agenda stage focuses on building the strategy, getting buy-in, getting stakeholders on board and ultimately agreement from the organisation to invest and move forward, remember that the communication about what you are trying to achieve, what outcomes you expect and what engagement you need from everyone is still not done. During the Prove Value stage you need to keep communication high, work to maintain engagement with your stakeholders and continue to educate the organisation.

The strategy and roadmap should be handled like marketing. Don't leave your strategy papers, slides, videos and infographics gathering dust. Get out to the wider organisation and continue the discussions, remind people of the plan, get champions on board with the journey, share progress updates, communicate the successes and what you've learned. Consider starting an internal newsletter. Add relevant news from your industry on how data and digital are being maximised, share stories about what's happening within the company, raise the profile of the team driving the agenda. How about running show and tell sessions in other people's team meetings or grabbing

---

28 B Onibalusi, 'Rule of 7: Skyrocket your business growth with this marketing principle', *Effective Business Ideas* (no date), www.effectivebusinessideas.com/the-rule-of-7, accessed 10 January 2025

a slot at the next board meeting? What about lunch and learn sessions to demonstrate early wins, data products in development or new insights that have been found? The power of easily shareable anecdotes at this stage is strong – use them brazenly.

Get it right and this communication essentially forms a sound basis for the literacy your people have around the use of data and AI, the confidence they have in the topic and the removal of fear that can creep in with innovation, change and uncertain times. This all helps to educate, increase understanding and get people behind what you're looking to achieve and the journey you are on. Telling people the strategy once then ploughing on will lose your stakeholders, restrict your ability to prove value and slow you down as you try to move to the Scale stage.

Iterate the roadmap

During Establish the Agenda you will have created a strategy for delivering value from data, identified the capabilities needed and assessed what the roadmap for implementing should be, based on the Level Up Framework. That will have given you enough to get the buy-in and investment required to move to this stage, Prove Value. It may not have answered all the questions and things may have changed – new CEO, global pandemic, strikes, someone in your team leaves. You will be learning more about your ability to engender change, conflicts or tension between teams, misalignment of priorities, further challenges on stakeholder engagement and so on.

During this Prove Value stage, alongside building a valuable use case, insights, team and platform you will also need to refine the strategy and roadmap. This will include prioritising the use cases and processes you will be focusing on as part of the next stage of your roadmap. This will allow you to focus on the right problems to solve, processes to fix or business opportunities to go after. Put these use cases into a backlog that can be easily communicated and managed, and placed on a timeline so you have a rough order in which you are likely to tackle them. This shouldn't act as a fixed plan but more as a direction of travel that gets reviewed on a regular basis to ensure the next use case to be worked on is indeed still priority and the right place to invest time, energy and money.

The capabilities required to deliver these use cases for the Scale stage also need refinement to ensure you have solid plans in place for your team, skills, culture, data governance and management, ways of working and technology. Your views may have adjusted through the delivery of your data product and rapid insights and your strategy and plans should reflect that. You are gearing up so that once you have successfully punched through from Prove Value to Scale, you know what to do next.

Most importantly, you need to further refine the investment required to get into and through the Scale stage, in which you push ahead with the delivery of business value and incrementally scale up your capabilities. This starts to require some bigger investments in people, technology and business change. Getting clarity on what's needed in terms of those investments and the expected value that will be returned helps to get enough funding to scale up your operation in a way that your stakeholders understand and are bought into. Build on the pitch deck that was used during the Establish the Agenda stage to get your initial funding. Show what you've been able to achieve, where you are on the journey, lessons you've learned, value you've added and most importantly where you are heading and the use cases you plan to focus on. This needs to be practical and tangible at this stage rather than visionary; you've moved beyond that. That's what will get your investment approved.

Update your pitch deck

During the Establish stage we talked about creating your pitch deck to lay out the story. You are now in a great position to go back with an updated pitch deck summarising progress but also including the validation points you have to back up the assumptions you'd made earlier. You'll also be using this to secure your next round of investment (this would likely be Series A in the world of start-ups) to see you through some or all of the Scale stage of the Level Up Framework. The table below shows the updated headings and descriptions that you should consider including in this latest budget request presentation.

Vision	A reminder of what you are looking to achieve and the value you expect to bring to the organisation. This is your why, your purpose for doing this, so is unlikely to have changed much.
Business opportunity	Update on the size of the prize you now expect to be able to deliver. You will have some better data to base this on now so can be more confident in your expectations and aspirations.
Early traction	This is an opportunity to summarise the value and learnings you've achieved during this stage. You can use your proof of value and tests you have carried out to show you have been able to deliver on the outcomes articulated last time. You can build some senior credibility through which you'll achieve the buy-in you need.
The problem	Provide an update on what challenges exist in the organisation that prevent you from being able to repeat, reuse, scale and ultimately continue to deliver the valuable outcomes that you've started proving. How far can you get with your existing team and what problems remain?

The solution	Cover how you will deliver more value and which capabilities you need to address to meet the business opportunity. What additional changes do you need to make to continue the positive journey?
Roadmap	Based on learnings to date, update the roadmap to show your plan for the next stage and beyond so it's clear what the journey looks like and what people can expect to see and when.
Investment needs	Now you are asking for investment to get through part or all of the next stage. Be clear on what this ask is, how far it gets you and what your expectations are of the returns.
Technology and platforms (optional)	Since a fair proportion of spend in data strategies is on technology and building platforms, it may be relevant (or required) to explain what choices have been made, what the end state looks like and how far along that journey you are. Some organisations will want to understand your position on cloud, for example, if this is a new concept.
The team (optional)	If you have already invested in new people or moved them around internally to create your initial team, it's often a great idea to introduce the team members and their backgrounds to build credibility that you have the right team (including your own background if this is you putting the case forward!).

Prove Value: The breakthrough criteria

There are some must-have outcomes you need to have reached to punch through to the Scale stage and ensure strong foundations are in place.

1. **Value delivered:** the most important criterion at this stage is that you have proven value to your organisation through delivery of a data and/or AI product against a use case (or set of use cases) and the delivery of key metrics.

2. **Refined strategy and priorities agreed:** you've built on the strategy and roadmap defined earlier in the journey and refined your focus and priorities.

3. **Organisational buy-in:** you have been able to develop the engagement with the stakeholders, build key allies and generate advocates for what you are trying to achieve.

4. **Minimum efficient organisation in place:** you have a foundational team in place who have helped you get through this stage and who can lead the implementation of the strategy through the Scale stage.

5. **Baseline technology platform implemented:** much of the value from data is enabled by a solid and scalable technology platform and architecture. Your baseline platform will need to be in place. You will also need clarity on how it scales to

support increased data, usage and complexity of requirement.

6. **Investment needed for the Scale stage:** you need to have secured budget to accelerate the development of the capabilities required to deliver against the use cases that support your business strategy.

7. **Your plan for the Scale stage:** you need a clear plan that explains what you will do in the early, mid and latter phases of the Scale stage.

PART 3

GROWTH AND IMPACT

When a start-up moves out of the early stages, they move into scale-up mode. They've developed and tested their proposition, they've got some decent investment behind them, they've built their MVP, had user feedback and started to build their community. They have traction but they aren't yet an established player in their industry. The scale-up mode is critical and focuses on continual innovation, improvements and accelerating growth.

In this part of the book we will be covering the remaining stages of the Level Up Framework – Scale, Accelerate and Optimise. This is your route to establishing data as a critical asset to your business and integrating AI into your operations, where you gradually build out the penetration of both into decision making and improving business outcomes. You've laid strong foundations in the first two stages and earned the right to continue that iterative development towards a capability that works with pace at scale across your organisation.

It's important to maintain the adaptable, agile and iterative approach through these stages. It's far easier to do that in the early stages when the scope is tight and the team and the investments are small. But the whole ethos of this approach requires you to ensure that you build your strategy around continual improvement, automation where possible, collaborative approaches to data and AI product development, and organisational change.

At the Scale and Accelerate stages of the Level Up Framework we also share what we call the breakthrough criteria, which act as a guide on what you want to achieve to punch through to the next stage successfully.

It's time to up the ante, get data on rails, have AI as an enabler and differentiator, and push on.

FOUR

Scale

We told the story earlier of Chesky and Gebbia, who tested their idea of offering out space in their apartment and proved it was a viable and valuable proposition. To get investment and scale the business, they needed to prove the idea would work. They needed to test several assumptions, like whether strangers would pay to stay in their home, and if strangers would let other strangers stay in their homes too. They had to use early prototypes to test those assumptions and use data and customer feedback to adjust and pivot their idea, the app and the proposition.

Once they had proven that the proposition would work and had a clear idea of what scaling would look like, they were able to secure investment, initially by joining Y Combinator's 2009 winter class and soon after that they received another $600,000 in a seed round from Sequoia Capital and Y Ventures.[29,30]

Then they were ready to put their foot to the floor and scale the business. The investment would help them to grow their team, build and test new features and integrations, grow the user base of their app and ultimately disrupt the market.

The Level Up Framework is designed to work in the same way. We urge you not to jump to this stage before you are ready because it's time to put your foot to the floor and scale your data strategy. You are building on the groundwork you put in place during the Establish and Prove Value stages and punching through the wall by hitting the breakthrough criteria. Unless you've done that successfully, there is real danger that you invest big but have missed crucial building blocks like buy-in, stakeholder engagement, a clear strategy and a credible path to success.

This is the meatiest stage of the framework. You are scaling up your team, your technology, the user base, the valuation and impact of your strategy, the features and functions your data and AI products provide and in the way that you operate. This takes time, energy, focus

29 M Brown, 'Airbnb: The growth story you didn't know', Growthhackers (no date), https://growthhackers.com/growth-studies/airbnb, accessed 10 January 2025

30 I Rabang, 'The Airbnb startup story: An odd tale of airbeds, cereal and ramen', *Bold Business* (31 May 2019), www.boldbusiness.com/society/airbnb-startup-story, accessed 10 January 2025

and commitment but sets you up for the next stage, Accelerate. Enjoy and keep that start-up spirit alive.

To self-service or not to self-service

To become an organisation that is guided by data and one where strategists, leaders and operators have the insight they need to make better decisions, it's easy to see why self-service becomes a panacea for many. The notion that a customer service team, the finance function and your head of HR can pick up their phone, open an app and get answers to their business questions doesn't feel like an unreasonable ask. After years of being dependent on another team (often the IT department), poor tools, slow response to requests and lack of true flexibility, business teams, as one board member put it to us, 'just want the data and we'll do it ourselves'. The win is huge here. Data, and more importantly insights, in the hands of people who can directly change the course of the business, the impact of a project and those making strategic and operational decisions is a sure-fire way of levelling up the returns you get. Yet this simple-sounding and transformational aspiration is more challenging than it appears, so the question is often raised of whether to implement a self-service approach or not.

Let's use an analogy. Prior to online banking, all the work was done for you. You asked someone to carry out an activity and they did the work to make it happen; even simple activities like checking your balance and transferring money required someone else to do that for you.

In 1981, four banks in New York City – Citibank, Chase Manhattan, Chemical Bank and Manufacturers Hanover – tested an innovative way of doing your personal banking through remote services, which made 'home banking' access available for the first time. In 1983, The Bank of Scotland provided its customers with the first ever UK internet banking service, called Home-link, which allowed people to connect to the internet to pay bills and transfer money. Self-service banking was born. By 2006, 80% of US banks offered banking over the internet and by 2020 more than three-quarters of British people used online banking.[31, 32] This had risen to 87% of the UK adult population by 2024[33] and 78% in the US.[34]

Even going into a physical branch, we rarely interact with someone else to carry out everyday banking needs. The self-service shift has happened.

Think about the work that must have gone into this shift. The technology changes, the maturity of processes, the

31 J England, 'Technology in Fintech and the story of Online Banking', *Fintech Magazine* (8 June 2022), https://fintechmagazine.com/banking/fintech-timelines-and-the-story-of-online-banking, accessed 10 February 2025

32 Census 2021, 'Internet access – households and individuals, Great Britain: 2020', Office for National Statistics (7 August 2020), www.ons.gov.uk/peoplepopulationandcommunity/householdcharacteristics/homeinternetandsocialmediausage/bulletins/internetaccesshouseholdsandindividuals/2020, accessed 10 February 2025

33 S Barber, M Boyle, 'Digital banking statistics 2025: How many Brits use online banking?', Finder (9 January 2025), www.finder.com/uk/digital-banking-statistics, accessed 10 January 2025

34 A Hrubenja, '25 online banking statistics for a financially sound 2025', Moneyzine (31 January 2024), https://moneyzine.com/banking/online-banking-statistics, accessed 10 January 2025

automation of data processing, the integration between banks, the global internet infrastructure upgrades, the regulation changes, and so on. Bigger still, how about the cultural shift needed to move people away from visiting branches to doing everything themselves online and through an app? This has required a huge level of education, messaging and marketing to ensure everyone understands how this new self-service approach works. Customer service and technical support teams are on hand to help when things go wrong yet even today many less digitally savvy banking customers struggle to make the shift away from their local branch to carry out transactions. That's a lot of change over thirty years to make this happen.

We aren't saying you need thirty years to move to self-service but we are saying that simply buying a self-service analytics tool or just giving people the data is not going to produce the results you expect overnight without a clear strategy, approach and plan for all the other things talked about in this book.

This doesn't mean it's impossible and that you shouldn't attempt it. Quite the opposite. However, it's a little more nuanced than full self-service or no self-service at all. It's good to think about this in the context of the three main modes business teams can engage with data, insights and AI models:

1. **Do it yourself:** business teams can build and carry out the necessary analysis themselves. In this

mode the team has all the tools they need, access to the source data, models and algorithms, clear guidance on best practice and rules of engagement. They understand how to apply data to business decisions and technical skills to make that happen. This is the highest level of self-service.

2. **Do it together:** business teams collaborate with data and insight experts to build and carry out the analysis together. In this mode the team may have some of what's needed in their own team, but not everything. Working on the elements they can and collaborating with others where necessary is effective. For example, dashboards are built by the business team, but data modelling is carried out by someone else. This is a hybrid self-service model.

3. **Do it for me:** business requests analysis and another team does it for them. The outputs produced would be self-served but the creation of them is not self-serve at all.

The beauty of understanding these modes is that it does not need to be one size fits all in your organisation – self-service or no self-service. You can make that decision based on the capability and maturity of each individual or team in isolation and set yourself up so that anyone can engage with data and insights in a way that suits their current or planned modus operandi. Like at school where students learn through different approaches – text, visual, learning through play, examples, reading, watching – the ways people engage with data should be based on their preferences and aspirations.

The other angle to consider is the introduction of GenAI tools, in particular so-called 'co-pilot' tools. These are intelligent assistants designed to work alongside us humans, enhancing our capabilities and productivity. You can think of them as digital buddies that help you with various tasks, from drafting emails and generating creative content, to analysing data and providing insights.

These tools are built to understand and respond to natural language, which makes interactions intuitive and efficient. Tools like Microsoft Copilot, Claude AI, ChatGPT and Gemini fall into this category. These are essentially self-service tools ready to go straight out the box, ready for people to use. The roll out of these inside organisations should be considered in the strategy for putting capability in the hands of the business.

Therefore, this isn't really a question of self-service or no self-service, but rather of deciding which is the best way to set ourselves up so that we have the greatest chance of making informed decisions through the application and guidance of data. It's about how we deploy tools, solutions, data and AI products advantageously.

The decision about which mode to be in should be made in conjunction with your organisational designs and operating model that will have been set and iterated through the journey. Which team works in which mode will also change over the course of your journey and that is fine – it should be expected and planned for.

Agility × collaboration = adaptability

The traditional approaches of project management for data projects that are fixed around agreed business cases, requirements, designs and outcomes can no longer support the rapid pace of change. If we are looking to create a business that can adapt by using data, insights and AI, we need our approach to be much more adaptable, agile and collaborative.

The shift in mindset and approach from big programmes of work and projects to sharp, outcome-focused development of data and AI products is consistently proved to scale better and at the right pace, deliver quicker results and increase collaboration between data and business functions. We need to move from a project-centric approach to a product-centric approach.

Earlier we defined product management as the practice of strategically driving the development, launch and continual support and improvement of your organisation's data and AI products. We defined a data product as a finished good that exists to solve a customer need, has features and KPIs and is iterated and managed by a product manager. Get used to these terms and think about how they can be applied to your business, as they help to think about your outcomes and approach to delivering those outcomes differently.

Improving data products should be an 'always on' activity, not a one-off development project that then moves to pure support mode. This may change the way you fund the development of solutions, which is typically a lump of capital expenditure (CAPEX) and then a smaller operating expenditure (OPEX) for several years. That CAPEX investment may be smaller and run for longer as you build and iterate your data products, or you may switch to a pure OPEX model to continually fund the creation of value.

This product-centric approach relies heavily on a huge increase in cooperation and collaboration through cross-functional teams that can work together to achieve an outcome and then continue to do so to iterate the product further. We have summarised the differences between cooperation and collaboration in the table below.

The difference is important. If everything is done with collaboration then you run the risk of an echo chamber, limited diversity in thinking and lack of creativity. If everything is done with cooperation then you may find that people go off in different directions, cracks appear and ultimately discord emerges between the teams that are allegedly cooperating.

While each on their own is important, to really drive value we need to focus on creating a culture of collaboration and cooperation between individuals, teams and organisations. This is a fundamental cultural norm that is required to be successful with data in your organisation.

Cooperation	Collaboration
Mutual respect	Mutual trust
Transparency	Vulnerability
Shared goals	Shared values
Independent	Interdependent
Short term	Long term
Sharing ideas from individuals	Generating ideas together

Set up your team for scaling

We have discussed the need to think about data in terms of products and services. For these to be created and implemented, you will need people with the right capabilities. We have grouped together data jobs to allow you to start thinking about capabilities. They provide a great guideline for thinking about what type of capabilities you have, what you may need to obtain and what training to provide existing employees.

The table below summarises the key roles split by disciplines. The exact titles and role definitions should be tailored to your individual organisation, but it's important that disciplines and roles are covered, based on the stage of your journey.

Discipline	Role	Role summary
Leadership	CDO (or senior data leader)	Leader for data. Generalist with good communication and problem-solving skills. Breaks organisational silos. May sit on the board.
Business discovery	Product manager	Responsible for the direction-setting and tracking of the roadmap for data products, plus leads the products themselves.
	Systems analyst	Technical understanding of the systems and platforms; helps ensure this is represented in data products and solutions.
	Process analyst	Specialism is the ability to manage and document process. This should also include the ability to track data flows aligned to process.
	Business analyst	An all-encompassing role that undertakes system, process and data analysis to help shape data products.
	Business engagement lead	Tracks and manages the value for data-related activity. Relationship role working closely with business stakeholders to help ensure value realisation.

Discipline	Role	Role summary
Delivery	Solution architect	Designs end-to-end and integrated data platforms that form the basis of all data work within an organisation.
	Data architect	Creates data models and related schemas. Purpose is to drive better information through reusable data sets.
	Data engineer	Designs and builds data pipelines to extract and transform a wide range of data sets.
	Software engineer	Specialist developer in big data tools and languages to build data pipelines, automations and advanced data processing.
	AI/ML engineer	An engineer who manages and monitors AI and ML models in production environments.
	DataOps engineer	Focused on enabling the rapid delivery of quality data products. Responsible for the set-up of and adherence to an end-to-end tool chain that allows for process control and automation across the data value chain.
	Data scientist	Responsible for deriving insights by using scientific methods, processes and algorithms to solve business challenges.

	Business intelligence developer	Responsible for creating reports and dashboards for others to consume.
	Analyst	Creates reports, dashboards and new analysis to help make business decisions.
Data management	Data value management manager	Responsible for setting the policies, standards and assuring best practice data management and governance approaches. Also tracks and measures value extracted from data activity.
	Data quality manager	Specialist in configuring data quality tools and assisting the business in using them.
	Data security manager	Ensures data is secure and access controlled to enable and manage risks associated with managing data.

Depending on the priorities in your organisation, you may not need all the capabilities immediately. The best example of this is hiring a data scientist. Unless you have robust reusable data sets, have ownership in place and are progressively using a consistent approach to data management, the hiring of a data scientist is probably not your highest priority. You may hire one or two if you have budget to understand the issues you need to resolve if you want to scale, but it will be more important to ensure you have a data engineer to support their work or make it clear they need to pick up more than simply the specific stated responsibilities of a data engineer.

That said, initially we tend to find it beneficial to hire people who are generalists and can do more than one role. In previous organisations we have looked at each individual and assigned them up to three roles. For example, one person could have data quality manager, analyst and data architect. It allows you to understand your existing workforce, plan training, look at cross-fertilisation or understand coverage. It also helps you understand where your immediate hiring need is. We have always found it useful to start small and hire on a 'just in time' basis. This may sound risky but bringing on board many new hires is time-consuming and can distract from execution. The balance is an art, not a science. The key is to ensure you have a clear roadmap in place to determine which services and products are needed and when they will be delivered. This way you can ensure that you have the right resources focused on the right activities.

Of course, having people with the right skills is great, but if they are not adaptable and willing to learn and change, then you need to look at your skills bench. For example, you may have someone in the team that is focused on implementing data management tools and practices to improve customer data. If you are to scale successfully, you will need them to also be able to develop and manage relationships across the business, be commercially minded, curious and pragmatic, able to tell stories and articulate benefits. This way, they can be consultative, sit side by side with business leaders and operational teams, and embed themselves in the organisation and outcomes of the business.

Likewise, if you have a data analyst in the finance function or operations department, for example, you'd want them to be able not only to get their head down and do some analysis, but also to think strategically, act operationally and engage with those in a central data function, IT department and a senior audience to make sure the benefit of their work is maximised. It is therefore important to create a team mentality in individuals so that they can work cross-functionally to get the best result for the organisation – no business problems or solutions happen in isolation, so it makes sense.

Not everyone is ready to work in this way or has these broader skills, of course, so it may be that this mindset needs to be built over time. For example, if your data scientist is not comfortable with presenting results to broader business teams or others outside their immediate team, then buddy them up with someone who can develop and coach their softer skills. If you are a data leader, ensure you give your team opportunities to grow, and in the meantime protect them, take the slack and make sure you provide the support and mentoring to put them on an upward trajectory.

One thing to note is that being in the Scale stage, doesn't always equal the need for more people; in fact, scale can often mean more is automated and therefore more efficient, so having a clear understanding of where there is bloat, where you can drive cost efficiencies in what you do and where you can deploy automation, you can be ready to scale back headcount if necessary.

Equally, we advise you don't scale teams in isolation. Data should be used to connect and drive understanding of how your organisation transacts. Scaling is not just about one specific team; it is about balance and timing. Being pragmatic about what the business really needs today, and in the future, and setting the team up in a way that most effectively gets the right results is what's important.

This is often the hardest skill to develop. Think customer first, organisational objectives second and individual team third. All work and interact with each other, but that lens helps you to make the right choices about the team. Finally, always use the test and learn approach. In a fast-changing environment, you will need to be adaptive and move in line with both your internal ecosystem and the environment in which it operates.

Keep the lights on

It is critical to ensure you understand how to declutter your team and operate at minimum capacity to keep the business running. It's good risk management. It is therefore important to understand what your 'keep the lights on' team looks like.

You may have budget and everything in place to scale, but you need to know how you will scale back if there are circumstances that change the status quo. We have seen and worked in organisations where scaling was undertaken with no real cross-coordination and over time people, processes and systems developed on their own. Imagine an ecosystem where you did not understand the dependencies and the impact of not maintaining equilibrium. It would become unbalanced and unsustainable. Business is exactly like this, and while evolution does not always mean scale, it does mean change.

Taking a step back and looking at the 'keep the lights on' team can also provide a fresh perspective and highlight inefficiencies. No one is above coasting when things are going great. Being prepared for the down times is easier if you understand the dependencies. Undertaking regular assessments on capabilities or people, tools and processes allows you to scale effectively and declutter if cost reduction becomes a priority.

This also assists with re-engineering and simplification of your organisation.

Developing the skills required

Go too early and you risk developing skills that can't be deployed. Go too late and investment in the other foundations can go to waste. Developing talent in the right order, at the right time and in the right way is a craft that becomes critical during the Scale stage.

If you refer back to the data value chain shown in Part 1, you'll see that data has a lifecycle: created, value added to it, value realised from it. Through that lifecycle, data goes from a raw material without much value, to insights and models that drive decision and change. Each stage of this lifecycle potentially requires some development of your team's skills, depending on what they have today.

How do we capture data in the right way and why is that important? What do we need to consider when building new technology platforms to ensure we manage data in the right way? How do we interpret reports to understand what they're telling us? How do we use data to tell the right story that drives action?

How do we have the confidence needed to base our decisions on data? What does it mean to 'be digital'? What does an AI-driven future look like?

These are all questions that need to be considered when you're developing talent and skill. Without the right understanding and skills, you can't shift culture, you can't take appropriate actions, you can't create the right mindsets and behaviours, and you can't maximise the value that's available from data.

Greg Freeman, leader in data literacy and culture, and founder of the market-leading Data Literacy Academy, says:

> 'The last decade has seen businesses of all shapes and sizes spend millions on data transformation, new technologies, and now AI. However, the key to unlocking value from all of that investment is taking your people on the journey and arming them with the skills they need to thrive.
>
> 'Until business leaders can close the two-sided knowledge and communications gaps that exist between data and business professionals, they'll never be able to fully enable data, insights and AI in their organisations. The coming years are critical, as they are about readying your people for a world augmented by data and AI, which is why data literacy, skills and culture are a vital cog!'[35]

---

35 Interview with Greg Freeman, 9 November 2024

From rigid to cross-functional organisational design

Traditional organisational structures – with rigid roles and responsibilities, boundaries around what teams can and can't get involved with, putting people, skills or teams in pigeon-holes and assuming they are unable to contribute to an agenda outside of their core skillset – hinder rather than enable you to develop an adaptable strategy and business.

Prior to the Scale stage, what's really needed are small, focused, autonomous squads that are able to apply their full attention to proving value, building credibility and delivering outcomes. If successful, this can lay the path for sticking to that kind of approach to the delivery and evolution of your data strategy.

When scaling we need to think about how we roll this concept up and out to ensure the organisation can maximise data and the outcomes it can achieve. We need to determine the best structure that allows for devolved decision making based on quality insights. To do that we need to focus the right people and skills at the right business challenges and opportunities.

It's therefore time to move away from restricting ourselves around teams based on functional roles or capabilities. Often you will have data engineers in one team (eg IT), data scientists in another team (eg marketing), analysts in another team (eg business intelligence team in finance) and those making the changes in a business unit (eg operations). Data solutions are built by passing the baton from one team to the next, each only concerning themselves with their functional skill and part of the process. Each of these teams will be measuring themselves on completion and quality of their technical process and not on the end goal of improving an outcome for the business.

This creates bottlenecks, silos, management overhead to coordinate across the teams, lack of clarity on where issues have occurred and why, and increased importance of up-front documentation and specifications to ensure each team knows their responsibilities. This leads to inefficient delivery and reduction in pace. The result? Limited business value, missed opportunities and questions from the board about what happened to all the great ideas and investment for a better tomorrow that never arrived.

The Spotify model was first introduced by Henrik Kniberg and Anders Ivarsson in 2012.[36] It is a people-driven approach to scaling that prioritises culture and the people network which focuses on autonomy, communication, accountability and quality. At the time, this was a radical approach but it helped them and other organisations increase their level of innovation and productivity. Since then this approach has been the bedrock of agile digital transformations and

---

36 M Cruth, 'Discover the Spotify model', Atlassian (no date), www. atlassian.com/agile/agile-at-scale/spotify, accessed 10 January 2025

how Spotify scales its product development and business. Much has been written about the pros and cons of this method; copying it to the letter is not always the best approach, but there is much to learn from it.

In the data world this approach is in its infancy, but it is already proving to be a big differentiator in building an adaptable organisation that can rapidly build, deploy and get value from data products. We need to take the approach to building a data product shown during the Prove Value stage: cross-functional, multi-disciplined teams (or squads) set up to focus on an outcome and apply that to all the data products we want to build and outcomes we want to create. Even though the squads should focus on outcomes, it is important that specialists within that squad (such as data engineers, data scientists and analysts) align and collaborate on best practices to ensure consistency and high levels of quality in that discipline. You can do this by forming capability hubs, typically led by a senior specialist who is responsible for setting standards, defining best practice and assuring adherence to that.

All that said, it would be naïve to believe that this level of cross-functional collaboration, hierarchy flattening and flexibility is easy to achieve in an established business. For many this requires a transformational shift in culture and mindset in how teams work together and projects are delivered. Not all businesses have a culture that can easily pivot to this approach. We can't all behave like a start-up and it's difficult to let go of current models. On the way to this new way of working you may need to make some iterations (fix one, fix two, fix three and so on) as you move towards that goal.

In the meantime (or alongside the concepts shown above), there are three recommended approaches to how you organise the teams and capabilities in your organisation:

1. **Centralised:** bring all the skills related to data and AI inside your organisation into a central team who manage and deliver all the data work required, working closely with those that need it. This can be a great model for organisations looking to bring control, consistency, best practice, alignment and increased quality to the work they are doing. But this model has the potential to create an organisational bottleneck as all requirements and requests go through a single team.

2. **Distributed:** skills are spread across the organisation in different departments, geographies and business units who build their own capability and focus on their own outcomes. This is a good model for those in global and siloed businesses and often where there are multiple profit and loss (P&L) responsibilities and therefore limited sharing of resource. The 'watch out' is that there can be high levels of duplication, limited efficiency in capability and technology investments and lack of coordination on business priorities and focus.

3. **Hybrid:** in this model (often called 'hub and spoke') there are elements of centralisation through the creation of a central 'hub' and elements of distribution through the creation of 'spokes'. The role of the hub is to set and manage the strategic direction for data and AI, plus support the spokes with tools, standards and ways of working, while also providing thought leadership and insight. It must focus on delivering value and prioritisation of resources to deliver this change. The spokes' role is to focus on the needs of the business unit they are serving – the last mile, if you like. They will continue to focus on their local needs, but will work with and to the standards provided by the hub.

All of these models can work and all have challenges. None are right or wrong and effectiveness can often come down to your start point, implementation success, culture and timing. All the models need skills, clarity, education, processes and collaboration. There is a line from very centralised to very distributed and you will need to work out where is best on that line for you, now and in the future.

Finally, it's a surprise to many to learn that any of these models can work for any organisation. While you may think that centralising is for smaller organisations and those that consider themselves beginners, distributed is for global and those that are advanced, and hybrid is for those in the middle, this isn't strictly true.

Netflix, a highly advanced, highly global and highly distributed organisation, took the decision to centralise its data function and capabilities. Elizabeth Stone, Netflix's chief technology officer, says:

> '...at the scale of company that Netflix now is, often data-oriented teams are embedded in other parts of the business, and we've resisted that and kept a centralised team.'[37]

Whichever model you choose, we urge you to use the squads approach to ensure cross-functional, outcome-focused teams working to solve real business problems. It is also necessary to engender a culture of collaboration and cooperation to achieve maximum value from these structures.

Value-driven prioritisation

Steve Jobs famously said, 'Deciding what not to do is as important as deciding what to do.'[38]

It's hard turning what look like good ideas down – it's a skill and it requires a process and practice. To achieve the level of collaboration, cooperation and

---

37 L Rachitsky, 'How Netflix builds a culture of excellence', Lenny's Podcast (22 February 2024), www.lennysnewsletter.com/p/how-netflix-builds-a-culture-of-excellence, accessed 10 January 2025

38 W Isaacson, 'The real leadership lessons of Steve Jobs', *Harvard Business Review* (2012), https://hbr.org/2012/04/the-real-leadership-lessons-of-steve-jobs, accessed 10 January 2025

focus on outcomes defined in the previous section, we need to improve how we prioritise the work that is (and isn't) done. Focusing on priority outcomes helps us be clear about what we're trying to achieve and keeps us doing the things that add value.

As a noun, 'value' is 'the regard that something is held to deserve; the importance, worth or usefulness of something', for example, 'the support you gave me was of great value'. As a verb, value means to estimate or calculate the monetary worth of something, for example, 'That data product is valued at £100,000 to our company.'[39]

Both these definitions hold true when discussing data and AI in an organisation as it can strongly value the people who contribute to the improvements of a business and apply a monetary value to what it is doing. From a prioritisation perspective it is important that both are considered. We value the opinions of people and what the data is saying but also the monetary return we think we will (or would like to) get. This is why it can be challenging to make priority decisions in an organisation.

Have you heard of the HiPPO theory? You are in a meeting with a bunch of your directors, discussing the options for European expansion. The countries you could start with, the product market fit in

---

39 Definition of 'value', Oxford English Dictionary, www.lexico.com/definition/value, accessed 10 January 2025

different areas, the local cultures to consider, whether the marketing metrics you use in your country will work across Europe. You're making good progress, unpicking the options, considering the data, discussing the bets and close to finalising when a senior director comes into the meeting and explains which country they have decided to launch in the following financial year. Job done, decision made and what they say goes. Does this sound familiar?

HiPPO stands for the 'highest paid person's opinion' and the theory goes that the opinion of the person who is paid the most or is most senior holds more weight than others. Their opinion is often the one that gets taken forward, even in situations where this may not be the right choice. The HiPPO theory describes an organisation's reliance on the instinct of humans rather than data in the decision making process. This is essentially the anti-approach to the whole ethos of creating a data-guided organisation.

Value-driven prioritisation is an approach that allows you to quickly measure an investment, a project, a change or an idea against the alternatives (including 'do nothing') and assess it against the overarching objectives of the organisation. It's based on the idea that we want to be working on the things that we know add most value, the biggest trusted wins, and avoid the things that drain cost, take uncalculated risks and aren't based on an objective assessment of potential (or known) upside. Sounds obvious but many organisations still don't assess the investments they make in this way. We're talking about creating a business that is guided by data; this starts with having a data-guided approach to prioritisation.

We need a mechanism for assessing value and for assessing priority based on that value. There are many different best practice models that exist for this such as RICE (reach, impact, confidence, effort), value vs effort, the MoSCoW method (must, should, could, would) and so on. Any of these can work if implemented well but the one we like that is pragmatic, simple to understand and easy to carry out is a 'business value vs ability to execute' matrix that compares how much value a product, project or outcome can deliver (business value) against an organisation's ability to deliver on it based on available funds, skills, technology, data, appetite and so on (ability to execute / feasibility).

As shown in the diagram below, the items that are high value and high feasibility should be a priority. For the ones with high value and low feasibility, we should consider carrying out tests that validate the value and show whether we can improve the ability to execute. Those items that are low value and low ability to execute we want to avoid, but those that are low value but feasible we should consider closely and proceed with caution. The sum of many of those may equal more than any individual item.

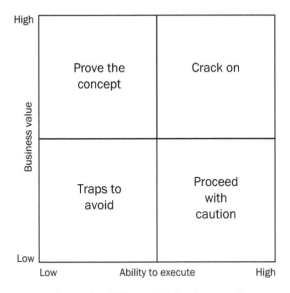

Value to feasibility prioritisation matrix

Building an adaptable data platform

During the Prove Value stage we discussed putting in place a starter technology platform that allows you to prove some value-adding use cases and build credibility. Once you hit the Scale stage you should look to iterate on that platform and build out an end-to-end ecosystem that meets your requirements and the pace of change. At this stage, much of the investment of time, energy and resources is spent on building out your data platform by consolidating and modelling data sets, building data products, building AI products and integrating these products into your organisation.

Adaptability is a common thread in scaling your strategy and ability to deliver incremental business value. The concept of levelling up is about constantly reviewing where you are, what's ahead of you and delivering value. This adaptability in the technology space is just as vital. What you need in those early stages of the journey, versus what you need as you scale, versus what you need once you hit a fully 'on rails' strategy is going to change. We talked earlier about the importance of aligning your data platform technology and design to your defined use cases. In reality you are not going to be able to predict everything and things will change. It would be impossible to define every use case you will ever need to deliver up front because your business is going to grow, your needs are going to adjust and the priorities will shift. You need to be in a position where your platform can adapt to that change without a total rebuild each time or needing vast investments to lift and shift from one technology to another. From a technology and design point of view you will need to be adaptable and you will need an adaptable data platform.

What do we mean by a data platform? You may hear terms like data warehouses, data lakes, data management platforms, data lake houses, data marts, data stores, customer insight platforms, big data platforms and many others. The market and the industry are rife with terminology and many of these terms have differing definitions but are used interchangeably.

To simplify things, we prefer the term data platform. We use this to mean the end-to-end ecosystem of tools, technologies and architecture required to ingest, store, manage, secure, model, interact with and use data. Within that there are individual components but to most people those components aren't important. What's important is that they have the tools required for them to deliver value to your organisation.

There is plenty of technology in the market from the established players (for example Amazon, Microsoft, Google, Tableau, IBM, Informatica) to the newer entrants that have made a splash (Snowflake, DataRobot, Databricks) to the start-ups trying to gain traction, particularly in the AI space. When you look at the marketing, it can be confusing to understand what part of the data ecosystem the technologies fit into and they all end up sounding the same. It's important to properly understand what you need at this stage of the Level Up Framework and what technology gaps you need to plug to satisfy your objectives. Go looking for vendors and technology solutions that fit one or more of your needs and that are aligned to your overall technology strategy.

To do this, you need to consider six key themes to ensure your platform has the right components and is adaptable.

1. Scalable architecture

You will want an architecture that allows you to start small, think and plan big and add capabilities over time in a way that doesn't back you into a corner. The architecture will need to cover the ingestion of data sets in batch and/or real time; the storage of data at various levels of consolidation, aggregation and modelling; the governance of the data platform for security, access controls, and management; and the usage and exploitation of data through analysis, reporting, further system integration and provisioning of that data elsewhere.

We discussed those components during the Prove Value stage and that had scalability built into the thinking. At that stage it was about having a lightweight platform that enabled you to deliver initial data products to prove a concept and show value. Now we need to think about tightening up the decisions on technology and progressing the technology strategy so that you can add components as you need to, to prepare for the evolution and delivery of the required data and AI products and services.

By knowing what's coming in terms of needs, you are able to make better decisions on what technology you require and put it together in the most architecturally sound and scalable way. This helps you avoid building a Frankenstein's monster of a platform without thought by adding new components that don't fit together.

Cloud platforms have a huge part to play here. In reality this technology and the reduction in cost of storage has been the accelerant to creating agile and scalable architectures at an affordable price point. Cloud should certainly form part of your thinking and plans. Some are still hesitant due to concerns about privacy and ownership, so education is needed to enable organisations to utilise cloud effectively and with confidence. Moving to cloud will improve your ability to start small and scale along with your appetite and success.

The additional power of scalable architecture is that it allows you to better integrate external data sets and tools, as well as GenAI technologies such as OpenAI's ChatGPT and the other co-pilot tools in this space.

2. Fit-for-purpose data modelling

We are at a pivotal point in design and modelling methodologies. Technologies and platforms have moved on so greatly that the constraints that traditional data modelling techniques, such as Inmon and Kimball, were designed to avoid, for example storage and computing power, are either no longer constraints or the impact has been massively reduced.

These methodologies were designed through the 1980s and 1990s and widely adopted through the 2000s. They were hugely successful and are still used today but are no longer necessary in all instances for the use cases you are trying to deliver or the work-loads you need to manage. Since the technology has moved on so much and we can store, manipulate and analyse data at such volumes and complexity, we need some new design principles to cater for this new world.

There is no single methodology that is the gold stan-dard for modelling like there was back in the 1980s and 1990s, although in recent years, Data Vault and Data Mesh have been approaches used in an attempt to modernise data architectures. In any case, we believe that no single modelling approach is correct for everything you want to do, and instead like to take a step back from those data modelling paradigms and think about design principles and the conceptual architecture against three layers.

1. **Layer 1:** this layer, often called the 'raw', 'data lake' or 'bronze', is where you store unadulterated raw copies of your source data. You may refer to this layer as your data lake, which is often misused as a general term for a whole data platform. This layer is not the wild west; the data has been properly and carefully ingested, filed away and catalogued so we know what data we have, where it's from and how recent it is. This can be structured, unstructured or semi-structured data from your CRM system, website, finance system, HR system and even documents, pictures, images and video. Most users of data

will not need to access this layer but it is an important step in the process of managing and providing data.

2. **Layer 2:** this layer is often called 'base', 'silver' or 'data warehouse'. It is where you start to think about the structure of the data so it is more suited for presentation to analysts, dashboarding tools, data scientists, ML models and so on. You need to think here about how you design data models so they are suitable for consumption and not just broadly storage as they are in the raw layer. Here you start to consolidate data sets and apply business rules, logic, calculations, aggregations and cleansing to create an end product for the purposes of analysis. It is where your regular metrics are stored so you can report on them easily; it will allow you to answer business questions such as, 'How much revenue did we make in the Europe region last week?' or 'What was the top-ranking product in Customer A over the last twelve months compared to the previous twelve months?'

3. **Layer 3:** this layer is often called 'analytics', 'gold' or 'data mart'. It is where analytical and ML models are built and/or stored. For example, a predictive score based on certain customer attributes, a next best action model, a marketing attribution model or a demand plan algorithm. It can also be used for simplifications of the data and data models in the base layer to, for

example, provide a dashboard tool that provides self-service reporting capability to the finance department covering just the data sets that are relevant to them. It's about creating specific data outputs to suit specific business needs.

The names of these layers are often used interchangeably or one of the names, eg data lake, is used to refer to them all. This can cause confusion, but ultimately what's important is that the capabilities of each layer are set up, designed and modelled correctly to deliver the tier of needs at each level.

The modelling methodology used across these layers varies as the use case for each layer is different. The key tenets of the modelling you choose should be (1) optimise for the technology and platform you are using and (2) optimise for your user and your use case. These will give you the starting point for deciding the best way to store and access that data and the best way to model to suit the purpose. The way someone in the accounts payable team needs data shared with them will be different from the way a data scientist needs that same data, as their interactions and needs are different.

3. DataOps and MLOps

DataOps and MLOps are each a set of practices designed to streamline and automate the lifecycle of data models in the case of DataOps, and ML in the case of MLOps. They're about applying a product management mindset to rapidly deliver (or 'ship') high-quality products. This means moving from an idea to a product that works and is in use quickly, then being able to iterate and improve on that product efficiently. They are both built upon three main tenets.

Firstly, it means a modern software engineering approach that takes lessons from the well-established DevOps paradigm used in the development of digital products (applications, website, apps and so on) and applies them to the way we create data and ML products. This gives us a set of practices that work to automate and integrate the processes so we can build, test and release faster and more reliably. The term DevOps was formed by combining the words 'development' and 'operations' to bridge the gap between development and operations teams. However, DataOps is not to be confused with DevOps for data.

Secondly, it means an agile delivery methodology that provides a structure to define and implement products iteratively and incrementally where every stage of the development process aims to add value. It brings elements of continuous improvement by measuring progress and output and finding ways to improve what you do and how you do it. We talked earlier about the ceremonies and practices that form part of this agile method and how this approach prioritises outcomes, communication, collaboration and getting work done over micromanagement, big up-front planning and working in silos.

Thirdly, it means cross-functional teams focused on valuable outcomes, which is about putting what you are trying to achieve at the heart of everything. The cross-functional element of this tells us to organise our people and teams cross-functionally, collaborating and cooperating, rather than in function or skill silos. That cross-functional team will then be centred around developing a data product that solves a specific outcome. This moves away from the traditional approach of different functional capabilities such as data engineering, dashboard development and analysts playing tag at various stages of a project, passing the baton until someone at the other end tries to deliver value. Instead all those people work in a group, obsessing about delivering the outcome together.

These three tenets make up DataOps and MLOps and give us a way to create an adaptable and rapid approach to building data products and platforms. With AI there are a few additional elements to be aware of that need management due to the nuanced and unique way AI models work compared with traditional software and data solutions. This all makes up the facets of MLOps:

- **Model drift:** AI models can degrade over time as the data that originally trained the model becomes less representative of the real-world data that it encounters. This is known as 'drift' and means each model needs constant monitoring and updating to ensure it stays accurate and reliable.

- **Experimentation and iteration** to develop models. AI models tend to require a lot of tests to find the best algorithm, parameters and features to make them work. This process and the iterative nature of development mean a tight and robust version control mechanism is needed.

- **Scalability:** AI tends to need large volumes of data to carry out its computations at scale. Because of this, MLOps helps ensure you can scale efficiently.

- **Compliance, security and ethics:** AI models need to comply with regulatory requirements, security protocols and ethical standards, particularly given the sensitive nature of the data that is often used.

- **Automation:** Since AI needs updating, iterating and improving on a continuous basis, it's essential that you can automate the deployment of models. This means updates can be applied and the time to market is reduced.

4. Standardisation and reusable approaches

You can move quickly, adjust quickly and be adaptable by standardising wherever possible and having reusable approaches to building your data platform. This is about having consistency on how you do things and not reinventing the wheel each time. It allows you to add new people to a team and they can hit the ground running, be productive and work in a considered and aligned way. This helps with support-ability of the platform so that it's easier to unpick and fix problems if standard approaches have been used across everything. It simplifies the way you design, build and support your platform.

This should cut across: reusable data ingestion frame-works; your system configurations so you don't always need to write new code; how you handle auditing of the platform; the approach to and reporting of logging and error handling; the alerts that are produced and what information is given; and how you monitor the health of the platform and the quality of the data in there. All this should be created and managed with standardisation and reusability in mind.

There are a few layers of reusability to consider: (1) a single platform-wide way to deliver a certain activity, for example error handling always follows the same structure; (2) source type specific – the way we handle comma-separated value (CSV) files and SQL tables may be different but the concept is the same; (3) indi-vidual customisations that are specific to the problem that you are trying to solve.

5. Flexible data access

Access needs to be provided to data in numerous ways. Different people and processes within your organisation will require varying types of access to data. Some need finished dashboards with no flex-ibility, some need automated integrations between AI algorithms and customer applications, some need to be able to run their own queries and create new analysis, and some need a subset of data and to be guided around what it means. The different personas and processes drive access requirements and your approach to data access needs to be flexible.

The tools needed for each of those access approaches will differ. Unfortunately, it's not the case that you procure and implement PowerBI from Microsoft, for example, and that's all you need. That will facilitate some data access needs but not everything. It will cater for some of your reporting and dashboard needs but it won't be the best choice for real-time integra-tions between systems or embedded data widgets in a mobile app, for example. It will only get you so far on building data science models before you need a tool such as Alteryx or Dataiku.

Depending on the use case, a GenAI tool like ChatGPT may also need access to your data so that it can combine the knowledge it has in its large language model and data sitting behind the interface you see, with your own 'first party' data about your customers, products, transactions and so on. There needs to be a way to access that data from external tools like this.

Being flexible and open to different ways of providing access to data in a controlled, considered and pragmatic way will help make your data ecosystem and platform more valuable.

6. Lab and factory

The 'lab and factory' concept is sensitive to the need of organisations to balance operationally controlled and managed data environments with flexible environments that are used for experimentation and innovation. One of the things that makes a data platform adaptable is the ability to do both those things at the same time and for different people.

The lab gives you the freedom and flexibility to innovate, try new things such as test out data sets and try a new predictive model in a semi-governed environment, with a wide selection of tools available. It allows you to test and learn and only go forward with the things that add value. You can have multiple people with multiple lab environments to suit their own local needs.

The factory is an environment that is more tightly controlled by a dedicated team, with controls to govern changes, the technology that can be used and how it is accessed. It will have a more rigorous testing and validation cycle before any new products or code are released into the environment. Typically, your board, corporate or regular KPI reporting packs will come from this environment, as will any models or algorithms that are powering your marketing campaigns or personalisation on an app.

The critical element is the route you establish from the lab environment to the factory environment, often referred to as 'lab to live'. There is a danger you end up with lots of experiments all over the place and nothing working on rails, at scale or being used to improve the business, with no established route to do so. You can also inadvertently end up creating more silos, more stovepipes between people and data. It's important to agree an approach for going from lab to factory, which requires the team working together, technology to support this and processes agreed. DataOps and MLOps are agreed approaches that support this.

This language works well across the organisation (with non-technical or data people) and it resonates as it aligns to the metaphor of a laboratory for investigation, experimentation and testing, and a factory that has a set process, control and governance and ships out consistent, quality products.

Sorting out who owns the data

Most people will probably agree that knowing who owns what inside organisations can be ambiguous. How many meetings have you been in where people have said, 'Oh, I think John owns this' or 'Jill said she owns that'? It means nothing. Usually there's no way to record who owns what; there are no clear boundary conditions (ie where does ownership for a thing start and stop?) and no ongoing maintenance of ownership (ie the artefacts that ensure ownership are not fit for purpose and don't meet business or regulatory needs).

The impact of not having defined ownership is that you can end up with poor data quality, inefficient processes, missed deadlines, inaccurate reports, dangerous algorithms and arguments about why things went wrong! We've seen this create inefficient meetings, confusion on who is taking actions, misalignment of expectations and, frankly, chaos.

Regulation and individuals' rights

While data ownership has benefits beyond regulation and individuals' rights, it has in many ways been shaped by legal frameworks and regulations. They vary across different jurisdictions, but generally share common goals of protecting individual rights and ensuring data security.

At the heart of these frameworks are laws like the General Data Protection Regulation (GDPR) in the European Union and the California Consumer Privacy Act (CCPA) in the United States. These regulations establish stringent guidelines for how personal data should be collected, processed and stored, emphasising the need for transparency and consent. They grant individuals robust rights over their data, including the right to access, correct and delete personal information held by organisations.

Level up to process ownership

When we began to look at ownership for data, it became apparent that we couldn't just assign it to data. Data only exists because it's been created by something – a form was filled in, a product was bought on a website, a customer was set up in a CRM system – so to limit the definition of ownership to the data that was created and not the process that created it is to split responsibility in a detrimental way. Data has context and defining ownership is actually a fundamental driver of change.

When we think about data ownership, we have to think about and add process, as this gives the context or boundary conditions to the data. Therefore, there is a requirement for ownership to be specific to a process, to have some form of context, and be framed so that it is understood across the business. It's far easier for people to understand and buy into the need for an owner for the process of creating new products so we can sell them in our shops, than it is to agree ownership for who inputs the colour and dimensions of a product into a management system. It's the context of creating products and being able to sell them, the outcome we are after, that's important. Creating the data is just a means to an end in this example.

Ownership, a team sport

Given that data isn't created in a silo, but instead exists in the context of process, business actions, activities by people and the broader ecosystem in which your organisations sits, it's clear that the game of ownership likely needs to be played by all stakeholders. Looking after the data is not just on the shoulders of your IT or data function.

There are six types of owners you need to consider, all of whom impact on the quality and accessibility of data:

1. End-to-end process owner

2. Discrete process owner

3. Critical data owner

4. System owner

5. Data producer

6. Data consumer

It's important to note that any one individual may be wearing multiple ownership hats depending on the size of the organisation or team where data is being created or used.

End-to-end process owner

An end-to-end process owner oversees the entire life-cycle of a process, ensuring seamless integration and coordination across all sub-processes. They maintain the efficiency and effectiveness of the process and smooth operation of the entire workflow. For example, the supply chain director at a retailer would be responsible for the end-to-end supply chain processes.

Traditionally the issue with someone being the owner of an end-to-end process is the implication that they have sole accountability. However, it is not practical for an end-to-end owner to understand the detail of the full end-to-end process, as it will inevitably cross multiple teams of the organisation. Discrete process owners, therefore, work with the end-to-end process owner.

These conditions are provided to help ensure the accountability of the end-to-end process owner is supported and that data ownership is agreed accordingly:

- The process should be documented end to end to ensure that all critical steps are understood.

- If the process being documented forms part of a more complex process, the start and end points need to be clearly outlined and reference should be made to other key processes that are impacted.

- The business outcome and critical data need to be clearly identified in the process. The outcome of the documentation is to capture and understand the process and data, and allow this 'asset' to be available in a business glossary.

- Where an existing process has been documented, it can be referenced rather than repeated.

- Sign off needs to be clearly aligned to the specific role of the individual.

- Data quality breakpoints need to be clearly defined to ensure that data quality rules can be run across the process. This allows for appropriate assignment to correct issues when quality thresholds are not met.

Discrete process owner

A discrete process owner is responsible for a specific standalone process within a larger system. Their involvement is crucial for managing the tasks that require focused attention and often specific skills. They impact the system by enhancing performance and ensuring the quality of their process.

The approach for ownership is to identify the key process steps at a high level and assign owners to the discrete sub-processes that sit within them. The discrete process owner reports directly or indirectly to the end-to-end process owner. An example, continuing the supply chain theme, is the goods inwards manager who is responsible for all incoming deliveries into a warehouse and ensuring goods are checked thoroughly and handled with care.

This is shown in the figure below, where a process has been mapped with six key component parts. This process is coloured light grey. However, like data, end-to-end process is also contextual, and for a particular context the process may have other activities that need to be brought into scope and understood. The dark grey shapes represent the other activities, with the arrows indicating a further activity which is not yet understood.

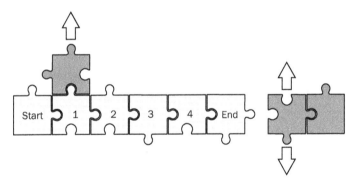

Ownership components process example

As process is joined and understood more broadly, the understanding of what happens in an organisation can be used to drive simplification and cost effectiveness. This is part of understanding the connections in your organisation, which will take time. Always start at a high level when documenting and get more detail as required. This ensures you can assign ownership quickly.

The other reason discrete ownership is important is that by understanding key breakpoints in a process and having an owner, you can assign actions where the data quality thresholds are not being met. This is a key part of the data management approach where data quality rules are run across a process.

Critical data owner

A critical data owner manages data that is vital for operational or strategic purposes as they relate to discrete and end-to-end processes. They ensure the accuracy, availability and security of this data, which is essential for operational efficiency, decision making and maintaining competitive advantages.

Critical data is identified through understanding the process that gives it context and makes it critical. The owner of critical data is required to ensure there is a simple definition that is maintained in a business glossary. They may also help define data quality thresholds in line with consumers and producers to ensure that the validity of data is appropriate. While there may be exceptions, assisting with data quality thresholds should be consistent.

System owner

System owners are responsible for the systems within an organisation's IT infrastructure that enable the processes to happen and capture the data. They are involved due to their technical expertise in maintaining system functionality and security. System owners may therefore look after your ERP, CRM, supply chain management (SCM) systems or any other applications used to run the business.

It is important to have systems owners assigned and these are usually, but not always, in the IT department. Note that IT does not own the data, but it does need to be identified, as the IT team is an important part of maintaining good data and enabling straight-through process. They maintain the responsibility for ensuring that systems are current, working and supporting business processes, and that systems and their controls are defined in line with business requirements.

Data consumer

A data consumer utilises data produced within or outside the organisation to make informed decisions or perform tasks. Their involvement is driven by their interaction with a process or their need for accurate and relevant information.

It is important that all consumers of data understand their responsibilities in transacting process and using data as it impacts on decision making and the operations of the business.

Data producer

A data producer generates data through various means such as transactions, interactions or observations. Their involvement is fundamental as they provide the raw data that organisations use operationally and strategically to run the business.

It is important, and often missed, that all producers of data understand their impact on a process and business outcome through the data that they produce. Without this clarity, the quality of data will drop and lead to broken processes and inaccurate reports. A person who sets up new products so they can be transacted in stores, per the earlier example, is a data producer for product data. The contact centre agent who writes down customer complaints is a data producer for customer data. The checkout assistant in a shop who puts the return codes into the till as part of a refund is a data producer for transactions. The impact of what these data producers do and how well they do it drives quality across the value chain of data.

Getting ownership right is actually a great way to drive a culture of collaboration and transparency in your organisation as there is an understanding and alignment on who does what and a feeling of shared ownership.

Scaling data management

The need for data management is clear and we have discussed this in a number of places in the book. How you approach data management is critical as you progress through the Level Up Framework. During Establish the Agenda, it's the time to get clear on the impact of poor data management and the prize for improving it. During Prove Value, as with everything in that stage, it's about creating momentum by finding some specific problems to solve, and solving them.

During the Scale stage, the focus is on scaling data management across, up and down the organisation, while remaining conscious of the need to invest carefully in the things that will add most impact.

Back when the CDO role first came into prevalence, in the aftermath of the financial crash in the early 2000s, the focus of the role, which we will discuss in detail in Chapter Seven, was on improving data management. Better data controls, better transparency, better reporting to the regulators became a big focus for organisations, led by the CDO.

This was and remains critical. Many frameworks, like the Data Management Body of Knowledge

(DMBOK) created by the Data Management Association (DAMA), provide comprehensive best practice, knowledge in data management, maturity assessment and practical implementation. For many, these frameworks have become their bible, and they should certainly be considered by those in the data management profession.

While these frameworks are a vital tool now and going forward, we have found over the years that they can be supplemented with a more practical and tailored approach that focuses on the strategic and operational implications of data management. One that is business-oriented to provide a more well-rounded perspective.

The elements of data management

There are six core elements to data management, each of which brings its own value and has its own set of disciplines. The points below show each element and the value it brings, and the table that follows shows the disciplines that sit within each element. Remember, the aim of all this is to make it easier and simpler for individuals and organisations to a) appropriately access and benefit from fit-for-purpose data as the basis of decision making, b) conduct business effectively and efficiently and c) meet regulatory obligations.

Valuable and actionable. Having data that delivers real business value and is actionable is achieved by ensuring data initiatives and actionable insights align to strategic goals. This is done by prioritising effort towards activities that directly contribute to growth, efficiency and risk management.

Trusted and reliable. Cultivating good-quality fit-for-purpose AI and ready, reusable and trusted data assets (such as customers, products, suppliers, employees) creates efficiency and is important for decision making.

Available and accessible. Making it easy to find and access data by processing and storing it in an organised way requires sound architectural design, seamless integration and democratised technology in the hands of the people running the business and making decisions.

Controlled and coordinated. Often called 'data governance', this element covers the need to have processes, roles, responsibilities and policies for how you manage your data ecosystem. It is an enabler for good data management and is required across the data value chain to ensure data is created, transformed, improved and used in the right way by the right people.

Ethical and compliant. Having and adhering to ethical standards and complying with regulatory obligations protects your reputation and avoids legal issues. This element ensures appropriate use of data which is legally compliant and aligns with your organisation's own values.

1. Valuable and actionable	2. Trusted and reliable	3. Available and accessible	4. Controlled and coordinated	5. Ethical and compliant	6. Efficient and automated
Data management use cases	Data quality management	Data architecture and modelling	Doctrine	Data security and access	Capability mapping
Value analysis	Quality quantification	Metadata	Roles and responsibilities	Data protection	Solution requirements
Business case/ funding	Remediation and enrichment	Data lifecycle	Organisation and operating model	Data privacy	Procurement
Planning and budgeting	Data quality performance	Reusable assets	Change management	Data legal and compliance	Solution assessment
Business and data strategy alignment	Data supply chain and sources	Ecosystem	Communication	Regulatory adherence	Solution support
Innovation	Traceability	Service performance	Auditing	Risk and issue management	

Efficient and automated. Technology is a fundamental enabler for great data management, so this element focuses on the right technology to automate and mechanise how you manage data efficiently and effectively. This helps to standardise what you do, making it more scalable and repeatable.

Within each of these elements are a number of disciplines that, over time and through the Scale and Accelerate stages, you should be looking to mature, aligned with your own strategy and needs.

Not all of these are required for your business, so the book won't be describing them in detail. The table simply serves as a reminder that there can be lots to consider in the data management space. We don't prescribe or promote the approach of programmes to implement all of the elements as an independent and standalone piece of work. Rather, align them to problems and use cases as described through the book.

Scale: The breakthrough criteria

In order to punch through to the Accelerate stage, there are some important outcomes you need to have reached so that you can ensure strong foundations are in place.

1. **Broad and deep value delivered:** the most important criterion is that you have delivered stated and articulated incremental business value through

the delivery of data products. This should be across a broad range of business areas and deep in several of them.

2. **Working on the top business priorities:** the efforts of those working on data products should be focused on the top three to five business priorities.

3. **Optimum efficient organisation:** you will need all the key skills required to operate a data strategy at scale. While you may have gaps in bandwidth, you should have no major gaps in capability by the end of this stage.

4. **High demand for data products:** you should have the problem of too much demand rather than trying to create demand. The main business units, functions and teams should be represented in your backlog of use cases.

5. **Embedded collaborative and efficient ways of working:** modern software engineering approaches, agile ways of working and cross-functional teams working on a business outcome should be well embedded.

6. **Data ownership and management processes in place:** questions over data ownership and how your core data is managed should be mostly ironed out.

7. **Investment needed for the Accelerate stage:** you need to have secured budget to move to the next stage of your journey.

8. **Your plan for the Accelerate stage:** you need a clear plan that explains what you will do through the Accelerate stage and changes that you will make.

FIVE

Accelerate

You should always be looking to move at pace, but by this stage it is about accelerating at scale. That's only possible if you have scaled on solid foundations through the previous stages. Poor foundations, poor value delivery or poor team organisation mean you cannot move fast or effectively. Poor execution of the previous stages seriously stunts your ability to accelerate and go broad and deep with the value data and AI consistently delivers.

Susanna Moan, CDO at electrical retailer Currys, has shown that focusing on establishing the agenda, proving value and being careful and value focused about scaling puts you in the best position to accelerate at scale.

'Investing in our data capabilities and delivering value along the way during the early 2020's has put us in a strong position to build on going forwards. In a varied economy, and with changing consumer behaviours, we're able to act and make decisions quickly based on insight. We can implement AI and it can act as an accelerator more quickly since we have strong foundations to build it on. We've been able to monetise our data by creating a service that returns income, in its own right. Aligning ourselves to the strategic and operational objectives of the business will continue to keep data at the heart of the business going forwards.'[40]

This stage, Accelerate, looks at some of the major capabilities and mindsets we've been discussing up to now, and at the considerations and adjustments you should make that allow you to accelerate at scale.

To accelerate at scale in practice

The points we have made around building data services and products and federating them into the organisation using an iterative approach are not just about building capabilities. They are there to ensure that as your organisation adopts the change you are building, it accepts that data is everyone's

---

40 Interview with Susanna Moan, 19 November 2024

responsibility and that this is about being able to make more decisions more often so that you can get things right for your organisation and its customers.

An ecosystem is complex and will always change because of internal and external influences. You may be accelerating different parts of the data estate based on your organisational needs, but you must understand that scaling other components requires scaling at pace. It is important that this does not become a 'technology or tools' project.

Let's use AI models as an example. Creating an AI model will require specialists in the data organisation, collaboration with engineering to build the right data pipelines and information security to ensure only the right people have access to data, and working with your data protection officer and product teams to ensure GDPR requirements are followed. The complexity cannot be ignored. We must ensure we have a clear rationale for the model. Its purpose is to speed up part of a customer journey by automating a decision.

If you follow the approach outlined in this book, you will have established all the data services and products needed. When undertaking the various MVPs, you're proving you have all the necessary components and that you can extract and measure value. It is also critical that you ensure the organisation is ready to change. If you have not considered the impact of the model you build to the operational processes, for example, implementing it will be difficult.

The model will not be static, so establishing relevant processes to manage and update it as part of business as usual (BAU) is also required. Once this has been done, you can use the test and learn approach to hone your implementation process.

This creates a conundrum for a lot of organisations. How do you invest in the change necessary to accelerate? Do you create a new organisation in tandem with running down the legacy? Where to start?

Part of the answer lies in selecting the right team. If you have analysed the people you have, started upskilling or hired the talent you don't have, then you are part way there. In Scale, you should have created the organisation, processes and products and services needed. If you haven't, then you are not ready to accelerate or move to the next stage, Optimise.

Let's assume this has been done. You should have implemented a number of data products and services multiple times by now. In each iteration of the implementation, you should have learned how to make the processes more robust and automated.

Accelerating is not just about automation and creating straight-through processing. It is also about creating detailed event-driven measurement. The ontology you developed will be maturing as you scale and understand the events you want to measure and how they relate to your customers or your internal organisation. This understanding brings the need for new metrics, more sophisticated analysis of data relationships and more data. You are now looking to automate, simplify and create a deeper understanding of how your organisation works and delivers to your customers. What your customers want and how they want it should also be a targeted outcome.

Accelerated decision making

In this book, making data-guided decisions has been a stated goal of the thinking of organisations. The building blocks you put in place during Establish the Agenda and Prove Value should set you up for sustainable and scalable decision making that you then put in place and iterated during the Scale phase.

At this stage, it's about accelerating your decision making, and more accurately, accelerating quality decisions. This comes from an understanding that the sooner insights can be acted upon, the more valuable they are; that insights should be integrated directly into algorithms, core applications and business processes; and that the insights we want to identify are complex and real-time.

It's worth recognising that not all decisions are created equal. Some require deep thought and consideration because of the size of their impact or the cost associated with the downstream activity related to the decision – R&D in a new drug, for example. Some decisions are small, easy to make and relatively simple to reverse, such as what to put in the marketing email to customers.

Either way, data plays an important part in making those decisions – data from previous activity that gives us insight to use alongside our experience and knowledge of what's happened before. The easier the data and insights are to access, the clearer they are in the message they tell us, and the quicker we can see the impact of our decisions, the better our decision making can become.

Without you actually making decisions and, importantly, taking action, all the thinking, work and investments you've put in place will be a waste. Make better, faster embedded decisions an objective for your organisation.

Technology evolution

We talked earlier about creating all the technology components needed to scale. These were broken down to allow for the necessary data and AI products and services to be aligned to business objectives. This assisted with planning what and when to create the infrastructure you needed to scale. If you have not created the components with the adaptability lens, then acceleration is not impossible but will be more expensive and take longer. The ability to build reusable and scalable components in the cloud makes this easier. Synchronisation of multiple cloud environments from different vendors, reducing reliance on one vendor or trying to only build open source all present issues that need to be managed.

Ensuring that the IT function understands the roadmap and functionality is critical. Many organisations forget that your technology stack is not forever. In building the components, you need to think like your team: 'What's the "keep the lights on" stack and what do I need to build now to ensure I can migrate off a vendor to another vendor or open-source application?' The technology stack will be continually evolving but at a pace that is cost effective and in line with other change.

Don't fall into the technology trap. There is never a single technology that solves everything, but if you scaled correctly, you may need to accept that payback on that investment means not upgrading your technology as often as you might like. There is always a place for innovation, but if your organisation thinks that a new technology that's come on to the market is the game changer to value and needed to go to the next level, then make sure you have thought about all the people, processes and change that are needed. Too often organisations assume that changing their technology will solve their problems, and the speed to delivery is undertaken without considering the broader organisation and environmental ecosystem.

Automation and rapid deployments

We have espoused the value of utilising process or customer journeys to understand data better and connect it to how you transact, while managing risk. The principles of collaboration, simplification and automation should now be second nature. To really accelerate, you have built the right products and services needed for delivery. Ownership is in place and activity is federated throughout your organisation. What is needed to take you to the next level?

The connection of your data products and services to the wider organisation and their delivery needs an effective approach. DataOps and MLOps, as discussed in an earlier chapter, are automated process-oriented methodologies for delivering rapid data and AI solutions. It's worth discussing them here in a little more detail as they're a real driver for acceleration.

The objective is to improve the quality and reduce the cycle time of data analytics. We take a broader view and are looking to create collaboration across the data lifecycle for all data, business, risk, operational and technology teams. This is not to be confused with the Agile approach to working. While using the Agile methodology to shorten the cycle time of analytics development is important, flexibility and adaptability in using these methodologies is needed.

For example, you may be utilising Six Sigma, a detailed and mathematical approach to process efficiency. Perhaps your project management has been codified and there are standards on good project management. While both of these approaches have value, they can also produce massive inefficiencies if used incorrectly. The same can be said for the use of Agile. You need to use the parts of the methodologies that make sense and work in your organisation's context.

Common sense, good leadership and the ability to make decisions are key. As long as you apply the test and learn philosophy, you should be able to move forward. While DataOps and MLOps have borrowed some of the principles and practices around continuous delivery and automated testing that were matured by DevOps, simply applying DevOps to data is not enough. DataOps and MLOps utilise statistical process control (SPC) to monitor and control the data analytics pipeline, ensuring that data is constantly managed and that AI models perform as expected.

We have discussed the need to build people and process to monitor analytical models in production. SPC is a part of that process. The good news is that SPC methodologies are not tied to a particular architecture, or technology, so can sit above the current toolset you have.

Automation to reduce cycle times and continually improve the data pipelines feeding analytical models and information delivery should be continuous. This includes fully utilising event data and driving automation into all processes. The introduction of more detailed triggers in process allows for automation of metrics to drive compliance with internal or external service level agreements. This is not without a cost. There will be legacy to decommission and you must bring your people along. The approach at this stage should be focused on automating everything you can. Make it as hands-free as possible and allow your valuable human resources to focus on true value-adding and decision making activities.

Building reusable components

We discussed the importance of standardisation and reusability being ways to make sure your platform can scale and be adaptable. However, reusability is broader than just your core platform.

When you're building your understanding about how your organisation connects, it is important that you can record, reuse and maintain the knowledge you've gathered. This will require not just culture change, but also a set of tools, and it is built around embedding cultural norms, being consistent with how you do things and finding ways to discover what you need.

An example of reusable components that support data management in terms of the relationship between tools, the organisation's existing systems and external data sources is shown in the diagram below. The different layers highlight the dependencies between these building blocks, which are a bit like the pieces of a jigsaw puzzle. Each reusable piece allows you to identify the different components that may be missing in your organisation's approach to managing data and information.

The key point here is that these parts are interdependent. The value and ability to map, understand, maintain and adapt your organisation are predicated on being able to connect and understand these parts. The building blocks must have the capabilities defined below to enable your organisation to capture, reuse and maintain the information. These building blocks are a simple way to ensure you build the right products and services and understand how the capabilities create a connected organisation.

It is also important to recognise the importance of connecting and recording the way your organisation transacts. This is great for auditing and regulatory compliance, and is just good governance.

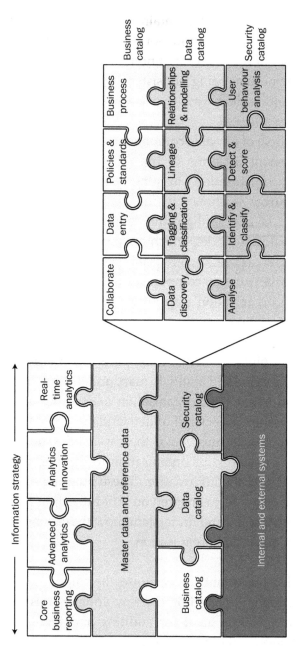

Reusable components and their interdependencies

For example, if you have defined some key personal data as critical, you will apply a set of standards to manage this data. It should be tagged with various attributes which could highlight destruction dates, type of sensitivity, etc. Then you will have clear business definitions and be able to see where in your systems and platforms it exists. You will have data quality rules to ensure it is correct and potentially be mastering the data too. Data flow will be linked to key processes using and creating the data. In addition you will have clear ownership assigned to the process, the system the data resides in and its definitions.

All these outputs are the result of focusing on reusability.

Refresh your organisation

Organisational change is hard, and the change needed to accelerate at scale is not just a data thing. Process changes will be needed to digitise the inputs captured when transacting, and in how you monitor and manage the outputs. Properly integrated AI has the potential to rewrite how you work, transform discrete processes or entire workflows, and disrupt your industry in ways that force some organisational realignment.

At this stage of the Level Up Framework, it's usual to need to look at the people you have, how they are organised and the work they do. Not just the people wholly responsible for data and AI, the data professionals, but potentially your business operating model more generally.

Data and AI talent

The skills of people in the organisation will change and need to be developed to create a more flexible and adaptable workforce that is attuned to using data to drive decision making and AI to accelerate and support their work. This may mean changing some of the people across your organisation, and while it sucks when you need to let good people go, if they won't or can't change in line with the new way of operating, it may be necessary.

For your people to work in certain new ways, strategic workforce planning is an organisational need and should be adopted by the entire organisation. This is born out of either the need to refresh the skills and mindsets or the real potential that AI means fewer or at least different people. The fear that AI will destroy jobs is a concern at a macro level, but it presents opportunities to create new jobs that we can't even imagine throughout the organisation.

Of course, it is optimal to keep internal knowledge about how your organisation works and the nuances and cultural norms that make it unique, so cultivating your existing workforce allows you to get the best of both worlds: a data-guided, AI-supported organisation, and a team that is reaching its personal and professional potential.

Using data to improve your data

Job families, position management, clear business hierarchies, current and maintained line management hierarchies are just some of the data inputs that shape what you need moving forward. It is important that you don't just focus on customer activity; you need to consider all the foundational capabilities that you require to run your business.

The good news is that this is not a zero sum game. Improving your basic reporting capability to have more reusable data sets needs some fundamental components, for example good finance data that can be linked to your employee population and sales data. An understanding of the cost of the entire organisation by geography, product and structure is needed to run an efficient business and can be used to make decisions about who you need where.

Data sets from employee surveys, performance reviews, absence stats and sickness levels all help build a picture of your organisation. As does understanding the skill profiles of the team you have, which can be mapped to what is required moving forward. Using data to help make these decisions, along with an understanding of what has worked in the past and your aspirations for the future, will really support the thinking and the story you tell to your organisation as you drive the change.

Continued culture shift

A close cousin of data and AI talent is culture. We've talked a lot about this through the book. The mindsets, behaviours and values your people hold as individuals and how that rolls up to the organisation either enables or inhibits your ability to move at pace.

You should have the picture now that your data team really is everyone in the organisation. Moving at pace is predicated on the fact that this is known, clear, understood and enacted. People across the data value chain recognise their responsibilities – obligations even – to create, add value to and realise the value of data and AI. In the next chapter, which focuses on the Optimise stage of the Level Up Framework, we feature organisations that look just like this, but for now, to get through to Optimise, we need to zoom attention in on assuring this culture and habit.

By the time you are through this Accelerate stage, you should have built not only the right tools, but also a team of the right people who operate in the right way, within the right culture that you have defined and expect. This is part of the ecosystem; you don't think about it, but understand its inherent value. The capture of how you operate is federated and the tools are part of the organisational fabric. Innovation and adaptability are key tenets of your culture and there is less silo thinking with more cooperation and collaboration. These things are not necessarily everywhere in the organisation, but they are the norm.

It is easy to take this all for granted, but pragmatism, collaboration and pace will need to be refined and maintained. As your organisation and the wider world evolve and change, the things you do to keep this culture also need to mature. That will keep you moving quickly at scale.

Culture change needs to happen both top down and bottom up in organisations. What is absolutely vital in Accelerate is that the leadership behaviours are such that they role model the culture you want and/or aspire to achieve. It's a clear signal of what is expected. It says 'We work this way' and this will be felt through the organisation.

Stop meetings where opinion and gut feel are winning over the use of data. Give business performance updates showing that changes to operations or strategy can be traced back to an insight you had that required you to do so. Use metrics to clarify why decisions need to be made, and then more metrics to show the success or failure of the outcomes. This demonstrable behaviour needs to be cultivated throughout this stage.

Monetising data externally

Much of what we have discussed in the book really focuses on monetising data internally. That is, treating data as one of the most valuable assets an organisation can possess and generating value from it in terms of meeting organisational objectives, whether they are improved revenue, better customer experiences, more efficient operations and so on.

If you think about organisations like Kantar, Experian and Bloomberg, they package up data, add value to it and sell it back to the industries in which they operate. However, it's not just data agencies like these that are able to do this. Monetising data externally presents a real opportunity for organisations to unlock new revenue streams and drive innovation, and once you have got past the Scale stage and into Accelerate, you are well placed to really consider this.

The allure of data monetisation lies in its ability to transform raw information into interesting insights that can be sold or shared with external entities because they add value over and above what they could gain themselves. This process can significantly enhance an organisation's financial health, but it requires a strategic approach. High-quality, well-organised data is the bedrock upon which successful monetisation is built. Without this foundation, the value of your data diminishes, and the potential for monetisation is compromised. This is why we urge you to ensure you have strength in the previous stages of the Level Up Framework in place first.

Understanding market demand is essential. Without this, you clearly have no opportunity for external monetisation of data. Through market research, you can identify potential buyers and their specific needs, guiding the development of valuable data products. You may be sitting on a goldmine of data that no one else in your sector has access to – product performance, market intelligence, history of transactions, customer insight and so on.

Regulatory compliance is another critical factor to consider. Adhering to laws such as GDPR or CCPA is crucial to avoid legal and financial repercussions for using data in ways it wasn't intended. Ethical considerations, such as respecting user privacy and obtaining consent, are fundamental to building trust and safeguarding against potential issues.

Once you have clarity on strong external data products, articulating the value proposition of that data set or those insights is key. Clearly communicating how your data provides unique insights or competitive advantages and having pricing strategies that reflect this value while remaining competitive is important.

Beyond financial gains, data monetisation can add value by driving internal innovation as it forces your organisation to think about and manage its data in ways you may not have considered without an end customer in mind. Selling your data or insights can give you R&D money to fund new projects and initiatives for internal benefit. It can also help you frame your data organisation in a different way internally, so you see it as a profit driver rather than a cost centre.

Monetising data externally offers great potential for organisations who are willing to navigate its complexities and those with a product mindset. It moves data to being a potential P&L item, which really changes the narrative of the value you can deliver.

Accelerate: The breakthrough criteria

To punch through to the Optimise stage, there are some important outcomes you need to have reached to ensure strong foundations are in place.

1. **Value alignment:** the organisation now has a clear proxy or set of metrics that are used as part of the planning process. Value is measured and calculated robustly, not made up or slashed to meet a target.

2. **Data-guided:** the organisation is now mature in its thinking about data and its part in success. There are no debates about 'why' and data is what the organisation focuses on.

3. **Data and business strategy aligned:** there is no longer a standalone data and/or AI strategy; it is amalgamated or fundamentally interconnected with the business strategy and the plan to implement it. Process work is synonymous with data flows and digital enablement. The strategy is connected and focused.

4. **Prioritisation pragmatism:** the silos in the organisation are weak and there is clarity on what takes priority. Change is managed in a mature and logical manner. There are clear plans and an understanding of the independencies that exist for the change to be executed.

5. **Organisational agility:** the capability of people can be utilised effectively. This could mean cross-functional teams, scaled agility or whatever works in your organisation. It does not need to include by-the-book methodologies.

6. **People capability:** the right balance of capabilities is in place. This forms a key part of the employee experience and is a foundation of the culture. Employees are challenged to develop in line with the organisation's needs.

7. **Ecosystem clarity:** you have connected and continually re-engineered how things are done to embed straight-through processing, AI automation and robotics process automation. This simplifies what is done and ensures that data can be gathered to continually adapt as stream

analytics continues to build the view on how you transact.

8. **Technology is effective and flexible:** technology has matured to create the right platform for innovation and fine-tuning data flows, integration of AI models and development of new data products to meet business needs.

SIX

Optimise

Over the last decade more and more digital-only businesses have been created and businesses with a physical foundation have invested in digital transformation. Those that succeed have used technology to change how they interact with their customers, manage their processes and think about innovation. The Optimise stage is reserved for the few that can behave like digital natives and big technology organisations leading the charge.

Introducing the data and AI native

Some of the biggest tech giants such as Facebook, Amazon, Google, Uber, Netflix, Apple and Spotify have built products and services that are underpinned by data and AI, and moved beyond the product and service we as consumers engage with. Their product is really their data and their AI-powered platforms.

In the UK, back in 2021, Gousto was valued at more than $1 billion, one of only a few businesses to do this in the food and drink sector. Gousto supplies subscribers with recipe kit boxes including everything you need to cook individual and easy-to-follow recipes. Founder and CEO Timo Boldt markets his company on LinkedIn as 'a data company that loves food'.[41] This is a top-down message saying 'We are data'.

These are no longer just digital native organisations but 'data native'. Data is at the heart of what they do and at the core of their product. In many cases, data is the product. The customer experience is enhanced with data. Improvements in operational efficiency are made with data. The data they have about us as consumers is used to drive our engagement with their services and their brand. They optimise their business and performance with data. Data and insight aren't reserved for a few people in data teams, they are baked into the fabric of the company. Decisions are routinely made with data. They have reached the 'absorbed' stage of the data pervasiveness scale mentioned in Part 1.

Similarly, AI-native organisations are the ones that fully integrate AI into their core operations, culture and strategy. Think of organisations like Tesla, which

---

41 Timo Boldt profile, https://uk.linkedin.com/in/timo-boldt

integrates AI deeply, particularly in its autonomous driving technology. The company's AI-driven approach to vehicle automation and energy solutions really demonstrates how AI can be central to a business model.

Unlike traditional companies that may adopt AI tools as an add-on, AI-native organisations are built around AI from the ground up. This means that AI is not just a tool to help out, but a central component of their business model, driving decision making, innovation and efficiency.

AI-native organisations leverage AI to automate processes, gain insights from data and enhance customer experiences. They often employ advanced ML algorithms, natural language processing and other AI technologies to stay ahead of the competition. Typically, AI-native companies are agile, data-driven and continuously evolving, as they use AI to adapt to market changes and customer needs in real time.

Moreover, the workforce in an AI-native organisation is usually skilled in AI and data science, fostering a culture of continuous learning and innovation. These companies prioritise ethical AI practices, ensuring transparency, fairness and accountability in their AI systems.

In essence, you could say that an AI-native organisation is one that has deep integration of AI into every aspect of its operations, making it a leader in innovation and efficiency.

The final stage

The Optimise stage of the Level Up Framework is about reaching this panacea. It is reserved for the few but you can get there. Organisations that start life as digital and data native get there quickly. You may see elements of this happening throughout the journey but at this stage it is fully absorbed. We are optimising everything in the business through the use of data. There is no end state of this stage. The key is to keep your organisation growing, maturing, fighting and ensuring you don't see decline. Organisations that reach here tend to have innovation at their core and a mindset of continual improvements and marginal gains.

Being at this stage doesn't mean you are perfect by a long stretch. You might still make mistakes, make the wrong decisions and have poor business performance for sustained periods. If anything, it increases the expectations your stakeholders and customers have and how much you are held to account for the way data is used.

However, more good is done by organisations who are at this stage to impact the world, society and individuals. Many positive things can come from being a data-guided organisation and one where data is absorbed into the fabric of the business, its products and services. We can put data to work on some of the world's biggest problems and challenges. We can put the smartest minds with the best data sets and change things for the better. We can create a business and societal ecosystem that exists positively, in balance and corrects itself for the benefit of all. That's our hope.

And because of this, unlike the other stages of the Level Up Framework, Optimise has no 'breakthrough criteria'. In essence, once here it's an ongoing iteration and reset, no next stage to break through to as such.

Data native story: SportPursuit

SportPursuit is a UK-based inspiration-led shopping club for deal-seeking outdoor and sports enthusiasts. It is a fast-paced scale-up that is currently adding more than a million new members a year. This is no luck or coincidence but down to a well-crafted and focused team who live and breathe the idea of being a data-guided organisation.

Co-founder and chief data and marketing officer, Victoria Walton, says that:

> 'We use data everywhere. Every single person uses data to do their job. We are truly powered by data and the information we use makes us highly attuned to our customers' wants, needs and desires and ultimately has given us our success.'[42]

---

42 Interview with Victoria Walton, 21 December 2020

While data has been used to help grow the top line, SportPursuit has been able to do this without adding cost by applying smart insights into the things that would ordinarily drive cost in a traditional, or less data-savvy, retailer.

Data is at the heart of decisions. They use data to recruit cohorts of members, targeting their paid advertising spend at people with the potential to become high-spending customers over their lifetime. They have a model that predicts each customer's lifetime value based on the first three days' worth of interactions with SportPursuit. They feed the forecast data into their advertisers to help deliver more of the right sort of people to SportPursuit's website.

Marketing spend is focused only on recruiting new members. Proprietary personalised CRM is then used to deliver long-term engagement from existing members, who continue to spend year after year, therefore delivering best in class customer acquisition cost (CAC) lifetime value (LTV).

They also use data to help determine their ranging and choice between their diverse stock models they have set up to ensure they are only buying products they know will sell based on the knowledge they have of their customer base. Victoria explains that 'the way we choose to buy is data-driven – understanding what has worked historically and what will deliver what our customers want. That knowledge comes from not only transactions but also purchase intent by customers and customers like them.'

SportPursuit has mastered the art of using data to guide decisions by applying human smarts in setting assumptions and using experience to tweak logic. This is done at an executive level; the senior team look at models, adjust how they work, monitor cohorts of customers and assess whether they are behaving as expected (based on data) and make strategic and operational decisions based on what they see and hear.

Some of the core models they use today were built in the very first months of the business being set up. This hasn't been retrofitted – Victoria says:

> 'It's been baked into the core fabric of the business from day one. It means we can hold ourselves to account, avoid lying to ourselves, avoid hiding from the bad news and focus on the granular KPIs in order to make better and sound decisions. Daily.'[43]

New joiners in the business are tested for their data savviness and how they think and learn, as they are critical components to the culture of the organisation.

SportPursuit is a perfect example of an organisation operating at the Optimise stage of the Level Up Framework. Data is in the DNA of the business, a core

---

43 Interview with Victoria Walton, 21 December 2020

part of how it operates. It is a data and digital native business growing because of the data it has and the way it is used.

Data native story: Gousto

Gousto is a British meal kit retailer that supplies subscribers with recipe kit boxes which include ready-measured, fresh ingredients along with easy-to-follow recipes. It was founded in June 2012 and is now serving six million monthly meal orders. At the time of writing, Gousto has achieved 'tech unicorn' status, meaning the business is valued at over $1 billion, following a recent investment round.

In order to become the nation's favourite way to eat dinner, Gousto needs to be able to provide the right level of choice to customers and create a customer experience that drives repeat use and subscription to their service. But, while Gousto is in the business of food, their founder and CEO Timo Boldt talks openly about actually being a data company that loves food. They wouldn't be able to do what they do, and grow as they have, without the innovative use of technology and data. Using data, and particularly artificial intelligence, is central to their business strategy.

This has been at the heart of the business and culture since the start of their journey. Boldt states: 'Data has been part of our DNA since day one.'[44] They know, have experienced and continue to see the importance of data. This manifests itself culturally across the organisation in two ways. First, the company has developed and makes extensive use of data products that are built and used in order to enhance the impact on the success of their products and, importantly, the end customer experience. Second, there is a strong emphasis on using rich information to guide their decision making, and culturally there is more than just acceptance of that but an expectation that decision making is backed with strong evidence.

Culturally, Gousto is a data first company. They hired data scientists early in their history, and have made extensive use of data science to accelerate their growth over time. They put data at the core of what they do and this mentality is felt across the business as much as at a leadership level. They have a strong appetite to optimise their products, their supply chain and the customer experience. The business looks to proactively identify problems to solve and collaborates closely with data scientists and engineers to apply data to those problems to rapidly test and solve issues.

Gousto uses data across their operation from creating a truly personalised service, from providing targeted and relevant recipe recommendations and forecasting likely demand to optimising the route that

---

44 Interview with Timo Boldt, 9 February 2021

products take around their factory and out the door to customers.

For example, Gousto is proud of its focus on giving customers variety each week in terms of the choice of menu. The company makes use of a 'data-driven menu' algorithm which optimises the recipes to display in a given week.

Within their supply chain, Gousto applies algorithms to drive operational efficiencies by optimising the routing of orders within its factories. Gousto has built data products to optimise the placement of ingredients in its factories, as well as the routing of orders within them, helping to increase throughput within its operation.

Gousto is also applying data science to create 'churn prediction models' that can identify customers likely to stop their subscription. From this information, marketing and customer care teams can react with relevant interventions through communications, offers and other means so that over time the customer interactions will become ever more personalised to focus on these customers.

Robert Barham, Gousto's Director of Data, emphasises that Gousto thinks long term about the data capabilities it needs to develop. 'Our starting point is our overall ambition several years out, and we work back from that to determine the data products we need to develop as well as the foundations that must be in place for them to be successful.'[45] This helps them deliver for today but also build the kind of leading edge data capability that enables them to continue to grow, act and behave the way they have by applying data to every decision they make.

They make excellent use of cross-functional teams across the business to ensure they have effective business, data and technology experience solving every challenge. Barham says 'the tribe model means we have clear domain boundaries as well as close collaboration between data scientists and other technical professionals – this helps us build products quickly and with maximum impact on our end customer.'

This is a business that has started with data at its core. They put learning and continuous improvement at the heart of what they do, and data forms a big part of their ability to learn and build a strong scalable business. Gousto's ambition in this space is infectious and they're a fantastic example of what it looks and feels like to be at the Optimise stage of the Level Up Framework.

---

45   Interview with Robert Barham, 9 February 2021

PART 4

DEFINING AND DELIVERING YOUR STRATEGY

While this book has frameworks you can use to develop your data strategy and work through the journey with pace, agility and certainty, we have focused more on the mindset and concepts that will allow you to achieve this. There are elements of 'how to' but we didn't intend for this to be a step-by-step guide.

This final part of the book is aimed at providing additional practical guidance on understanding where you are, defining your strategy and your journey, and on the role of the CDO. This section will help you plan, plot and track your journey, bringing together the advice from the rest of the book.

SEVEN
Plotting And Tracking Your Journey

The modern CDO

The CDO role was first established in the early 2000s, mainly driven by the rising importance of data governance and compliance following the 2008 credit crisis and increased financial regulation like the Sarbanes-Oxley Act. This meant the role was largely born out of the financial services sector with Capital One often being credited as having the first CDO.[46] In banks and insurance companies particularly, the role was appointed to enforce data governance and manage risks far more effectively.

---

46 MITLibraries, 'A Cubic Framework for the Chief Data Officer (CDO): Succeeding in a world of Big Data' (March 2014), https://dspace. mit.edu/bitstream/handle/1721.1/98915/Madnick_A%20cubic.pdf, accessed 10 January 2025

Soon the role was being heralded as a must-have not only in financial services, but across all industry sectors as organisations recognised the value and benefit of having a senior leader in charge of their data strategy and efforts. The role evolved from managing data to finding ways to leverage it for strategic advantage. This led to CDOs growing their focus across data strategy, quality and insights to support and drive business decisions.

Despite the role having grown substantially over the years, what has not improved is the clarity about what a CDO is responsible for. In many ways, despite its age, the CDO role is still immature, working out its path and hampered as much as it is helped by the continual hype around data, data science and AI.

While many executives and people in organisations have known they need to care about data since the CDO role's inception, they have seen multiple failed data programmes, adding costs to the business with limited clarity on the value delivered, and this continues to create questions about what a CDO is, what they should focus on and how they best add value.

Responsibilities of a CDO

From our personal experience in CDO roles, working with CDOs and having thousands of conversations with CDOs across the world, we have learned several key lessons about the role.

Let's start by laying out what we mean by a CDO. This is a senior member of the executive team, at or one layer below the executive committee. The role should have full responsibility for the definition and execution of an organisation's data strategy with a priority around delivering incremental business value tied to the strategic objectives of the business. We see a CDO as accountable for the data strategy and value extraction in a business, driving enablement across the organisation and leadership.

This is leadership for the development of people and for ensuring that a culture of utilising data is developed and matures over time. Leadership for the development of data products and services and ensuring strategy is aligned to business objectives. Leadership for breaking down silos and implementing a new way of working, utilising the necessary techniques like Lean, Agile and, most importantly, common sense.

This is a big ask. Having a technical understanding of data and the supporting technology is fundamental, but without good communication, resilience and a steely determination that data is the conduit to changing an organisation, the role becomes transactional.

If you think about board level positions, they all have strategic responsibility and ensure that operational efficiency is executed correctly. They are all business roles and are likely to have input with regulators and other third parties who form part of your broader ecosystem. The CDO, therefore, should be the same. A CDO is a key role if you are to mature and scale the data products and services necessary. Get a CDO who understands both strategically and operationally what's needed. Make them accountable for driving the data agenda. This includes aligning the strategy but also running and executing the MVPs to determine what your organisation needs to change. It requires establishing the roadmap and creating a plan for people, technology and change with the other leaders in your organisation, so it is a collaborative effort. If it is seen as a land grab then you need to adapt and change the narrative.

It is important to recognise that many organisations won't be large enough to have a CDO, so another role or roles may be needed. Regardless of organisation size, there should be someone in a data leadership position who has the remit, support and budget to engender change. The title is less important than the acknowledgement that data needs specialist skills to build a fit-for-purpose data ecosystem.

It's also important to recognise when a CDO isn't in fact a CDO at all. This is when they hold a head of data science, head of data and analytics, head of data governance or other such position. This is often the result of organisations wanting to say they have a CDO or data science team, but not really wanting to change. They like to look forward-thinking, but don't want the cultural shift needed to build a data ecosystem that can be scaled and optimised. This only comes from someone having the level of seniority or at least clout in the organisation to drive that change.

As you successfully move through the Level Up Framework, you will find that you bounce between the stages as you iterate and develop new products and services. Getting an organisation to change the way it operates is not a linear process, hence why we have emphasised the ecosystem complexity. At some point during the transition towards being data-guided, it is worth thinking about evolving the type of CDO you have and considering evolution and succession based on where you are on the journey and priority focus.

Background and behaviours of a CDO

A word of warning: having a token CDO is like having a paper cut-out person help you push an object up a steep hill. A CDO needs to have teeth, backing and influence.

Let's discuss the background and behaviours to look for in a CDO.

- **Strong business background:** The role of the CDO is a business role so the individual should be able to understand, communicate and challenge the customer. We don't see industry experience as critical – in fact, it is often useful to have someone come into this role with a diverse viewpoint. However, an understanding of business and the mechanics of how it operates is crucial.

- **Negotiator and communicator:** An ability to talk the language of IT, marketing, sales, finance, risk, HR and so on is critical to ensuring your CDO can gain credibility. They will also need to highlight the awkward idiosyncrasies of the organisation; how that is done can be fundamental to people understanding why things need to change. They will often need to disagree, challenge and disrupt, so their being able to do this without destroying relationships is vital.

- **Understands technology:** Regardless of what responsibilities they have for the infrastructure and technology of the organisation, your CDO needs to understand how it works. It is their job to challenge the experts so that the right architecture is delivered. This does not mean they need to be a deep expert, but rather understand what components are required and ensure those are built.

- **Collaborative and adaptive:** If your organisation is to build an approach that breaks down barriers and silos, then improving collaboration is important. The CDO needs to be able to work with and adapt around people up and down and across the organisations. The best ideas usually come when your teams are adapting to a challenge as it creates the spark to think differently.

- **Leadership:** Building the right team and getting them to support and challenge the organisation's approach is key. They need to be able to draw on their expertise and challenge the CDO to drive the right solution. It is the CDO's job to develop the individuals in the data team, and the culture and skills across the organisation. As a leader, they need the organisation to follow the path they outline. This means creating the links between people and processes and supporting the overall business objectives.

- **Listens and is pragmatic:** Your CDO being a partner to the rest of the organisation is predicated on them being able to understand what's really required. This comes from listening carefully. It is essential they continually question and fully understand issues. Doing a 180° turn and still moving broadly in the right direction is often how you achieve an objective. If everything were linear, the path to success would be simple. A CDO listening and then being pragmatic about solutions creates strong lasting behaviours in how things are done.

Regardless of the title and or who takes the responsibilities, these underlying behaviours help to ensure the right culture is created from the start of their tenure. You and they can then adapt to what is needed as you learn more about the journey.

Challenges faced by the CDO

Given the cross-cutting responsibilities of the role, the CDO faces some unique challenges in being accepted, making change happen and gaining recognition for the value they deliver. One of the most significant challenges for CDOs is overcoming resistance to change.

The transformation to become a data-guided organisation requires a cultural shift, which can often be met with scepticism or reluctance by employees who are used to traditional ways of working. CDOs must act as change agents, promoting data literacy and demonstrating the tangible benefits of data initiatives to gain buy-in from all levels of the organisation.

While we've articulated that a CDO should have a seat in the boardroom to influence strategic decisions, a second major challenge is securing that seat. Given CDO is a relatively new role and may not be fully understood by other executives, this challenge can be hard to navigate, particularly as the boardroom table is full of established positions already. CDOs need to clearly articulate the value of data and how it can drive business outcomes, positioning themselves as essential partners in the organisation's strategic planning.

Thirdly, unlike traditional business functions, data projects may not have impacts that are immediately visible or easily measurable. At least, not in a way that can be directly attributable to the work of data and analytics.

CDOs need to develop metrics and KPIs that demonstrate the ROI of data initiatives, such as cost savings, revenue growth or improved customer satisfaction. This helps in justifying investments in data infrastructure and analytics, but more importantly, it shows why their position is a value-adding one in the organisation. They also need to find ways to partner with other business leaders to deliver value together, as per earlier sections on aligning data products to business outcomes.

The next challenge relates to the complex landscape of global data regulations, such as the GDPR in Europe and the CCPA in the United States. CDOs need to navigate this landscape and ensure compliance with these regulations. This requires a deep understanding of legal requirements and the ability to implement robust data governance frameworks in partnership with other teams like legal, risk and security.

This is, of course, particularly challenging for multinational organisations that must comply with varying regulations across different jurisdictions. Given the global nature of customers for most businesses, this is broadly relevant to all organisations now.

Finally, a big challenge, and one that is in fact threatening the role of the CDO moving forward, is too much focus on the D. The data. Data on its own can help with operational improvements in the business, but it's really as it moves down the data value chain that the value is really felt. Using it to create information and insight and ultimately drive decisions is where the juice starts flowing.

Since many CDOs have focused on the data, it's opened the door for new roles to pop up, like the chief analytics officer (CAO), chief AI officer (CAIO) or combinations like the CDAIO in a bid to demonstrate it's about more than just the D. Organisations need to clarify the terms of reference and responsibilities of their CDO so that the scope of the role is clear.

The future of the CDO role

Today, the CDO role continues to evolve. Successful CDOs are increasingly seen as innovators and disrupters, driving change and digital transformation. They are responsible for curating a data-guided culture, promoting data literacy and identifying new revenue streams from data assets. As organisations recognise the value of data, the demand for skilled CDOs is expected to grow, with a focus on AI, other emerging technologies and strategies for monetising data externally.

If your CDO understands the business and has helped to manage the operations, risk, technology and data as an ecosystem that is connected, then as you plan your organisational people trajectory, it is worth thinking about how you create the increased understanding of data across your key leadership roles. This could mean your CFO becoming a CDO. Whatever the outcome, having a single leadership role for data is critical. It may mean that in your 'keep the lights on' structure, the CDO responsibilities are consumed by another C-level role. If the organisation has evolved, this won't mean the key responsibilities discussed above become less important.

If you are developing your CDO from your C-suite or team one level down from this, then make sure the person has the aptitude to understand all the components of the role. Just as a person can learn the risk frameworks, they can learn about the technology and data.

The technology is moving fast and there is not a static way to manage and connect your data. Your next CDO should be adaptable, resilient and good at connecting and understanding problems. They should think about data in terms of what the organisation wants to do with it – the products and services lens we have emphasised. As in any role, if you bring someone in to create momentum for change, they need to be the right fit; if they are an existing employee, make sure they are a disrupter.

Given the increasing importance of being digital and adaptable, there is an obvious question: where does a successful CDO go next? Do they stay as a CDO? With the value of data to improving the operations, they could take the seat of the chief product officer, chief operating officer or chief revenue officer. If they have a finance background and the necessary qualifications, then there is no reason why they couldn't become a CFO.

For some, there is definitely a path to becoming the next-generation data-guided CEO. If you are a CDO, this is certainly something to consider, and if you have one on your board, executive team or leadership team, then their progression could be a game changer for your organisation.

Six pillars of a data strategy

At any stage of your data journey you can take a step back and ensure you have a solid approach to data and AI in your organisation. By applying a clear and concise method to that assessment, you can articulate where you are, where you want to be and the gap that exists between those two states.

A data strategy is a framework that enables you to deliver business value through the application of data and analytics. You should define that strategy as a written artefact to help you articulate what you plan to achieve and how you will get there. This is your story, your plan and your communication tool wrapped into one.

The following six pillars bring together all the components required when writing your data strategy. Miss any one of these in your thinking, planning or execution and you will struggle to reach your full potential, limit opportunity and slow your progress.

Vision and value

Your vision should describe the important role data plays in achieving success for your organisation and the specific business value you hope to achieve by making decisions guided by data. Successful data strategies are purposeful, focused and restless in their attempt to deliver business outcomes.

This pillar also includes the articulation of what you are solving. By aligning to the business strategy, this pillar is where you identify the key pain points and opportunities (use cases) that exist in your business and through which data or AI can be applied to improve the decision making and create better solutions.

This is the place to assess the impact of AI on your organisation and the broader industry you trade in. Work out which business problems it is suitable to support and which it isn't. Highlight the areas for R&D and the areas for fast execution.

With this articulated, you can align the rest of the data strategy pillars to it and use this pillar as a way to engage, excite and generate buy-in for your strategy.

Key outputs: Vision statement, use cases prioritised based on the potential business return, information requirements (and how they map to use cases).

247

People and culture

Making decisions guided by data is about your people and the culture of your organisation. This pillar looks at the skills needed to be successful at implementing your strategy and how best to organise them. This needs to cover data, technical, AI, commercial, operational and management skills. It includes defining the roles and responsibilities of teams and the individuals within those teams and the education programme you may need to improve their data fluency, knowledge and capability.

This needs to be backed up by a culture of blending intuition, experience and insights. That doesn't happen by accident so in this pillar you will be defining what you can do to start changing the culture of the business. This starts with people – what they do, how they behave, their skills, the collaboration opportunities and sharing of knowledge and projects.

Key outputs: Skills required, skill gaps identified, target organisational structure, culture change activities identified and articulated.

Operating model

The approach used for prioritising, defining, delivering and managing with pace and agility can make or break your ability to deliver maximum returns from data. This pillar emphasises the importance of how your teams collaborate and cooperate with others to build data and AI products and deliver business outcomes.

This pillar should articulate which method you will use to prioritise the business outcomes to invest energy into on a BAU basis; how you allocate that work to the teams and squads you have set up; and the approach to building your data products and services to test ideas and scale the successful ones through to a live environment. It looks at how you involve the executive and/or senior leadership to keep them engaged, bought in and up to date with the status of the data strategy. It looks to embed a mechanism for measuring and monitoring progress at a macro strategy level and a micro projects and products level.

It should consider how you govern AI at a corporate level to ensure you are building it in a responsible way, inside the legal and compliance frameworks of the time and based on your own policies for how AI can be used. It's where the governance around the management of risks associated with AI is agreed.

Key outputs: Prioritisation framework, chosen delivery and management methodology, approach to project governance.

Technology and architecture

There are plenty of established and innovative technologies on the market. Your ability to onboard, embed and adapt your technology platform as part of your strategy is a huge differentiator and one that can get insight to the right people and help them create a stronger business.

This pillar looks at what technology you need in order to get hold of, manage and use data and AI effectively. It should define the technology strategy for your data tools and AI platforms and how they all integrate with the rest of your system landscape. It should look at assessing the architectural approaches that enable you to build successful data products at pace.

Key outputs: Technology strategy, technology capability gaps, architecture approach.

Data management

The key outcome of data management is to have trusted, secure, quality and well-managed data that is ready to be harnessed by humans and AI to make decisions and drive the business. Without this, organisations face the challenge of relying on low-quality, uncontrolled and untraceable data, which acts like a daily tax on your organisation and blocks the rest of your strategy.

This pillar identifies the work required to improve the level of trust in your data, starting with the definitions of your key business metrics, how they are calculated and who owns them. It should look at what data you have, how it's captured, how it moves through applications and who owns each data set. It should look at how you secure data physically and through strong access controls. This pillar also looks after the quality of your data and in particular how master data sets (like customer, products, assets and so on) are created and managed.

If you are in an industry that is bound by regulatory controls, this will also need to cover how you ensure that those controls are met, documented and communicated.

Key outputs: Decision on policies, standards, procedures, regulatory controls, data ownership plus creation of key metric and data catalogue.

Roadmap

A vision without a plan is just an idea. Your strategy is not complete without a clear picture of the stages you will go through to deliver business value and build the necessary capabilities. You need an agile and adaptable plan that allows you to communicate the journey and improve at pace.

This pillar is where you pull the other five pillars together into a roadmap for delivering your data products and AI solutions, and the order you should build out the capabilities required to help you meet your objectives. Importantly, it will articulate the culture change initiatives required to create a data-guided and AI-positive culture.

Key outputs: A single-page roadmap, backlog of deliverables and short-term actionable next steps.

As this is strategy and planning, there is no need to answer every single question or go into huge detail. Don't be tempted to stay in strategy forever but use it as a tool to make decisions on what you need to do and in what order.

This six-pillar approach has been successfully applied in the private, public and third sectors and in organisations from start-up to scale-up, small, medium and large enterprises. It has been successfully applied in single location, single product organisations and large multidisciplined, globally distributed organisations.

To see how you score against these six pillars, try using the Data Strategy Scorecard. Through a series of questions, it will unpick how successful your strategy is and provide you with a score and some tailored recommendations on where to focus your attention. Visit http://datastrategyscorecard.cynozure.com to take the test.

Relationship between data, information and business strategy

Part of the 'vision and value' pillar is about understanding the information your organisation needs. The delivery of information will be based on specific use cases and will be designed to support flexibility while driving cost efficiency, transparency and speed of delivery that meet internal and external demands. The information you need is built from the data you consolidate for different purposes. There are three types of data set you'll need to create:

1. 10 × 10 data sets: used for published and standardised reporting

2. 10 × 50 data sets: used for more detailed analysis and created to solve business problems or for more complex analysis and decisions

3. 50 × 50 data sets: used for training analytical models and building decision-focused models

These data sets should be prioritised based on the information needs of your organisation, which should be determined according to your business strategy. This ensures alignment of what your organisation is trying to achieve and how (business strategy) with the information required and business questions you need to answer (information strategy), and the data required to answer those questions.

The relationship between business strategy, information needs and data should be understood and defined and you will need to do this in a way that drives simplicity in the way you capture, store and use data. If we get this right, it allows us to shape a data ecosystem and platforms that mean you can deliver information based on the increasing complexity and range of data required against the following domains:

- **Core business reporting:** answers your business questions, serves up agreed metrics and meets any regulatory reporting you are required to do.

- **Advanced analytics:** provides outputs of models and algorithms that aim to solve business problems and deliver on opportunities through foresight and predictions. These will be iterated through 'analytics innovation' and may generate new metrics that feed into 'core business reporting'.

- **Analytics innovation:** explores new insights, metrics and predictions that are often experimental or one-off analysis. This information may or may not be published and may require ad hoc hierarchies and structures to be put in place.

- **Real-time analytics:** provides real-time operational information to run what will have become BAU activity in your organisation.

Each of these domains has a different set of characteristics about the data, how it's managed and the need for agility. The table below summarises those differences.

Domain	Veracity	Velocity	Volume	Variety	Mgmt	Agility
Core business reporting	High	Low	High	Low	High	Low
Advanced analytics	Low/mid	Mid/high	Mid/high	Mid/high	Low	High
Analytics innovation	Low/mid	Low/mid	Low/mid	Mid/high	Low	High
Real-time analytics	High	Very high	Low	Low/mid	High	High

Putting your data strategy together

At any stage of the Level Up Framework, you can take a step back and review your strategy to see whether it's still fit for purpose. Some of the pillars may need more of a focus than others but it is important to keep a close eye on all six to make sure your strategy is working for you. The difference comes from how much work there will be to (a) define your strategy and (b) implement the changes. This is all impacted by the external environment, changes in data leadership, changes in business strategy that will impact on your data strategy, and technology improvements in the market.

There are three main questions you are looking to answer in defining your data strategy:

1. What do you need to achieve against each of the six pillars (desired outcomes)?

2. Where are you today against each of the pillars (current state)?

3. How will you close the gap between the desired outcomes and the current state (activities)?

There is a tendency to focus on point two, the current state. This is often called a maturity assessment, capability assessment or health check. We don't advocate doing this as a standalone review because it doesn't give you a full picture. There is an element of 'so what?' about it. What your organisation really needs to know is: what will we do about it? What will we change? How will we get better and how will it impact our business?

It is best to approach this as a single set of activities to help you answer these questions in one efficient exercise that focuses on extracting maximum value from each interaction you have with your stakeholders. You will want to gather information from a cross-section of your organisation on its current ability to deliver value from data, the capabilities that exist and most importantly the business strategy you are trying to align the data strategy with. Be focused on what you are trying to achieve and know the purpose of conversations. It's easy to overload people with interviews and workshops about similar and overlapping topics and it's best to be empathetic and sensitive to people's time.

We also suggest running workshops with a cross-section of business stakeholders to identify the use cases required to deliver the business strategy, the size of the opportunity and the business questions that you would need to answer to plan for and deliver each of those use cases. These form the basis of the 'vision and value' pillar but are supplemented with the findings from the information-gathering stage.

You can then use your experience, data and judgement to articulate answers to those three key strategy questions. This book can help shape some of the approaches and options you have against those pillars. It's also important to lay out the short-term opportunities that you can crack on with, often referred to as 'quick wins' or 'low hanging fruit', as they pose an opportunity to start making a mark quickly. Be careful not to get drawn into only ever doing quick wins as this can become tactical. Make sure they contribute to the direction of travel you are outlining in the data strategy. Try to make conscious and communicated decisions rather than sleep-walking into new challenges that you'll need to clear up later.

We have seen organisations invest vast sums of money and months and months on an exercise like this. It doesn't need to be that way. For small and medium-sized organisations this should take between one and two months. For large organisations, possibly two and three months. This requires the right level of skill, experience and ability to cut through the noise and get to the point quickly.

Plotting the journey and building the roadmap

Once we've articulated the desired outcomes, the current state and the activities we need to put in place to close gaps, we are in a strong position to turn this into a plan for how the data strategy will be implemented and evolve over time. This is the sixth pillar of the data strategy, your roadmap.

The roadmap will be used to outline your expectations on when activities across the data strategy will be carried out and the order in which you will focus on the business use cases.

The roadmap isn't a fixed plan to be followed with precision but more a guide and expectation management tool. It provides important context for how the activities relate to each other and is realistic in its delivery of those activities. It needs to be responsive and adaptable to what happens as you progress and as the business evolves.

Take the full set of use cases and activities required under the data strategy pillars that you have defined and apply some prioritisation to ensure the most important and feasible things are worked on first and the dependencies between the activities. Once that is understood you can express them as initiatives in a timeline – this is your roadmap. The diagram below shows a simple and high-level one-page roadmap.

The planning horizon is down to you and should take into account budgeting cycles, visibility needs and

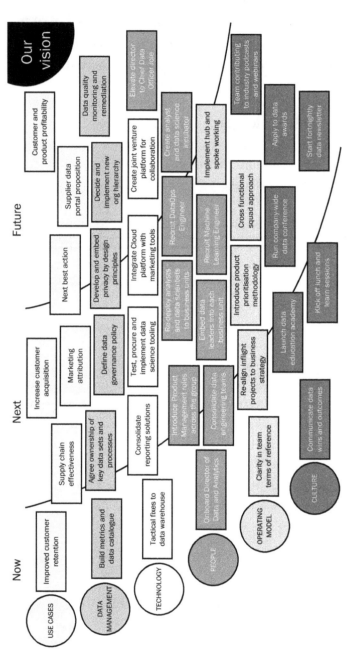

Example plan on a page data strategy roadmap

aspiration. The tints in the roadmap can be used to indicate which pillar that activity is associated with – this often helps to show the breadth of work required.

You can use this to easily and simply communicate the 'how' of your data strategy. This shows the important steps required to achieve your vision. For stakeholders who would benefit from seeing a summary of the plan without all the associated detail, this tool works well.

The Level Up Framework as a planning tool

The beauty of the Level Up Framework is that it can act as a tool, not only to ensure you have covered what's needed in each stage of your journey but also as a way of planning the implementation of your data strategy.

By using the guidance in this book and particularly the breakthrough criteria at the end of each stage, you can build a robust plan of what you will do, when you will do it and how long you expect things to take. You can map and align your activities against the stage you are at. You can then be clear on what outcomes you are expecting at each stage and mini milestones along the way.

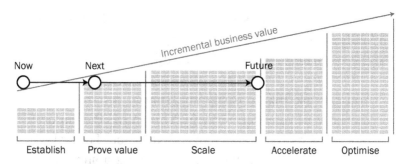

Level Up Framework states aligned to roadmap

You can use the language of this Level Up Framework day to day, to help articulate where you are and what's next. We have heard organisations say, 'We are establishing the agenda at the moment to get early investment to go and prove value,' or 'We are currently in Prove Value so the focus is on building credibility and minimum viable data products before we increase investment to scale this up.' This language helps psychologically to align the work you are doing to the stage you are at and the end point you are trying to achieve.

Measure and monitor progress

In the same way that this book talks about using data to get insight about your organisation and its performance and to ultimately guide decisions, you should also be putting in place an approach to measure, monitor and communicate the progress of your data strategy and your Level Up journey.

Why do we need to measure?

You have probably lost count of the number of times you have been asked, 'How is the data strategy going?' or questions to that effect. Before you know it, the answers 'Yes, not bad,' 'Getting there,' or 'Coming along!' are pouring out. Partly it depends on who is asking, the context and how formal the question is, but it is essential for the good of your strategy that you are able to articulate how it is performing in ways people can understand.

We are looking to understand whether we achieved what we set out to achieve (the outcomes), if we achieved it how we said we would (the approach) and the resources it took (time and cost). With regular retrospective reviews you can assess these questions and make decisions about changes you might need to make to your strategy and/or roadmap. These could result in short-term tweaks or longer-term adjustments but without proper assessment, measurement and data, it's difficult to make those decisions.

The act of measurement drives action. It raises accountability to the plan and commitments that have been made as part of a strategy or roadmap. Being involved with the measurement and seeing results drives increased transparency and communication, resulting in an increase in performance as everyone strives to improve outcomes. This measurement, done right, can get everyone rooting for success and aiming for a common goal that you can be proud of.

What do we need to measure?

A good measurement is one that supports the understanding needed to answer the question of how good or bad something is. It needs to encourage behaviours that have a positive effect on individuals, teams and the organisation. For that to happen the measures need to be simple to compile, clear and easy to understand. Each measure needs to be owned by someone so we know who has the responsibility to improve it.

In the case of data strategy we really should be looking to measure the following key metrics of success:

- Business outcomes of the data strategy

- Business outcomes of each data product put into action

- Costs incurred to deliver those outcomes

- Time taken to deliver those outcomes

- Throughput of data products and data product changes

In smaller organisations, where you have a clearer line of sight between activities and outcomes, this is more straightforward than a global team with siloed business units that have autonomy. Whatever your situation, there is huge benefit in a culture of capturing, measuring and communicating this in aggregate so you can ensure you are delivering value but also learning and adapting as you go.

Communicate and iterate

Communication and continual learning are at the heart of everything we have discussed in this book and form the basis of a strong data-guided culture. We should communicate and celebrate success and failure. Whatever happens, we have learned something and, if we have implemented the start-up mentality of starting small and growing the successes, we will have given ourselves a fighting chance of communicating successes more regularly. Communication is key. Transparency is vital to creating open and honest dialogue internally. Sometimes this will be uncomfortable but it allows you to move forward.

Refer back to your stakeholder map and create targeted segments of your audience to communicate to. Tailor that communication to suit the audience and pick the most appropriate medium to engage them. Some will be better in a one-to-one discussion, some prefer a report, some will need a team presentation. All of this helps with buy-in, clarity and collaboration.

A successful idea we have seen is to have an equivalent of the Golden Globes for your data strategy. How about the 'best use of data' award? The 'best improvement in query time' award? The 'best algorithm' award? The 'best newcomer' award? This less formal way of measuring success can help to engage your organisation and recognises great work and outcomes.

If you put communication at the heart of your strategy for planning, tracking and monitoring success, it will return in spades.

Reality check and looking forward

While we've shown the stages of the Level Up Framework as a step-by-step journey, it doesn't always turn out like this. People change, the environment changes, business strategy changes, technology moves on and what you think will work doesn't. You will probably take as many steps back as you do forward, need to change direction, start again, pivot and adjust. That's the point – it's about adaptability and building a culture and framework that allow (and celebrate) those things.

As things are never perfect and many aren't starting from a blank sheet of paper, some capabilities will be more advanced or behind than others. You could be at multiple stages of the Level Up Framework at once. Some parts of the data strategy may work better than others and be more progressed. This isn't a problem, but you should use the framework to bring everything in line.

You will need to revisit your data strategy multiple times to refresh it, re-communicate it and pivot it around change. You can use the guidance on building and refreshing a data strategy to check you have all your stages of improvement mapped out.

It's important that you can work with ambiguity. You won't have all the answers all the time. You will need to be adaptable, expect change and use change agents within your organisation.

Dealing with legacy and fixing forward

We wrote this book to push an agenda that ignores the trendy metaphors; for business people to understand that operating in silos, blaming IT and thinking data is a silver bullet for your organisational issues won't work. While we 100% believe that this approach is a winner, in reality it is only an 80% solution. Just as a great data scientist is needed to move from a correlated relationship to a causal relationship, good leadership is needed to move any organisation forward with this much change.

However, changing at pace is often held back by legacy technology and infrastructure, and at some point you will need to manage that legacy. Those organisations that have invested in dealing with legacy over the past five to ten years are in a much better position to attain the promise of AI benefits than those that are trying to put foundations in place now. New technology and legacy technology don't always play nice, so having an approach to dealing with legacy allows you to innovate and move forward.

Legacy is one of the biggest issues management faces. Keeping existing infrastructure running costs is not practical when most organisations need to reduce the expense line. The approach we recommend is not looking to create massive projects simply to turn off your legacy; it is doing that while building the right products and services to deliver value.

As you deliver more change, you reach a point of decommissioning of your legacy. We have seen this done the other way round where a company runs a project to 'lift and shift' from legacy on premise hardware to cloud technology. All they end up doing is moving the same mess from an old system to a new system.

Unless you know what you have in your systems and what it means, then any project to move to a new platform can create a program that is too big to succeed. It may sound easier just to move 'as is' but all you are doing is delaying the problem and creating a mess in your new platforms.

If you do not change anything you will continue to create more legacy and make the problem bigger and more complex. This is where we use fix forward.

Effectively fixing forward sees you draw a line in the sand. Fix forward is about setting a new mandate.

It establishes an edict that you are going to manage process, systems, data and behaviour differently. This change recognises it is necessary for you to create a data ecosystem that enables value for customers, shareholders, employees and regulators.

Fix forward is the start of your trek in using data to enable your organisational objectives. It helps you prioritise what you start on. By acknowledging you have a legacy issue and you need to change, you can scope the change. The next step will target an improvement to a BAU process or as part of an existing or new change initiative. You have not forgotten your legacy.

Part of the toolkit is having a clear set of data standards. Data standards form part of the consistent data management approach and are a reference point for decision making. We all know that policy and standards do not always translate into change. You will be surprised how quickly fix forward spreads in an organisation; its power is in saying: 'I am not going to fix everything, just the new thing I am doing.' Fix forward is also pragmatic in its application. You are not trying to achieve 100% compliance with data standards. You are looking to ensure that you adopt as quickly as possible new ways of working and reduce future legacy issues being created. How quickly you progress to align to the data standards will depend on the complexity of your organisation's legacy and the current culture.

The first and most obvious place to implement fix forward is in your change or transformation portfolio. This is often the place where you plan to resolve bad behaviours and create newness. At this point, you need a pragmatic review to assess what parts of the change portfolio need the right mindset to fix forward and correct poor habits and systems that are causing problems.

How many times have you heard a project manager say, 'Data is out of scope'? This must be one of the craziest statements that can be made since data is fundamental to every digital and technology project or process change. However, if there are no data standards and no understanding of what is needed from data, then it is understandable. Data is pervasive across an organisation. Fix forward helps you start afresh.

Having a policy and standards only goes some of the way; the key is being able to make a review based on the necessary data products and services that data will support. It's about stopping the 'data' conversation, which is almost esoteric in nature and easy to sidestep, and starting to talk about data outcomes – things you need from data. Examples include a data quality service, reference data service or lineage service; some data products include management reporting or a ML model accessed via a user-friendly app. Having a part of the solution is not good enough. That is why we provide a set of tools to allow you to understand what you need, when you need it and at what scale.

Neil Clutterbuck, chief underwriting officer at Allianz Insurance Plc, summarises their journey:

> 'Like many organisations we had tried to get our data estate in order – we recognised this was strategically important to us and that we were and continue to be a data rich organisation. We had invested in data, but our ability to derive the desired returns was proving a challenge, as too was co-ordinating activity across federated data teams. Our challenge was how to coordinate and extract value from our data ecosystem.

> 'After a couple of attempts to move ourselves forward we decided to try and tackle the problem differently and appointed a chief data officer. With a CDO on board we developed a plan to create the paradigm shift that we sought. The plan was comprehensive, covering not only the what and the how, but also the cultural shift needed. Delivering against that plan was not without its issues and was hard yards. But by fixing forward and investing in understanding the products and services we needed we started to build the capabilities we needed. We invested time and effort to communicate the "how and what" we needed to change and we

have progressively built and obtained value so that as an organisation we are aligned and looking to scale our capabilities. We can now exploit the value embedded in our data estate. This has been a great journey for our people and is allowing us to adapt and change at pace, just as the environment around us continues to rapidly evolve.'[47]

Fix forward is about unshackling from the past, mentally and physically. Drawing a line and giving yourself a chance of letting go and moving forward. It's easy to get busy fixing legacy; it can be a world of pain. Fix forward ensures you do not keep creating more legacy issues and allows you to change at a pace that works for your organisation. You will need to decommission, but fix forward is important to help you do that with sound foundations. It also ensures as you change, you build flexible, agile and adaptable systems in conjunction with organisation capability.

Business capability lens on your data ecosystem

In Part 1 of this book, we introduced business capability maps and how they can be used to a) understand the functions of your organisation and

---

47 Interview with Neil Clutterbuck, 2 December 2020

b) use that understanding to find opportunities for improving and applying data, insights and AI. We used an example of a manufacturing firm to paint the picture.

Over the last few years, we have been testing and iterating using this same capability approach to describe an organisation's data ecosystem. It's an alternative way to understand the capabilities needed to manage data and AI, and create data products and associated services. Just like the manufacturing firm can be broken down into business capabilities such as product development, supply chain management, manufacturing operations and so on, you can apply this approach to data.

There are the same rules here around the characteristics of the capabilities:

- They cannot be repeated; they are distinct.

- They are not a reflection of the organisation structure.

- They are descriptive. It is not about how something is done, but rather what is done.

- They can be both tangible and intangible.

- They are outcome oriented. Each capability needs a clear outcome.

The diagram below shows an example of what an ecosystem capabilities map might look like for an organisation. It is essentially a way of drawing out all the capabilities required, such as data integration and building dashboards and AI models, and grouping them into key areas that make up the data ecosystem. The specific areas and capabilities need to be named and aligned to the way your organisation operates, but in this example, the areas of the ecosystem where the data capabilities sit are broken down as follows:

- **Business data modelling**: Represents data through the business lens of your organisation

- **Data management**: The governance, processes, policies, guidelines, standards, controls, compliance and rules of how to manage data

- **Data source ecosystem**: The internal and external data which is available and interesting for consumers

- **Data integration**: Connects and moves data

- **Data layer**: For insights, analytics, models and sharing

- **Data access**: Authorisation and management of access to data

- **Data provisioning**: A way to link data and applications together

- **Search and consume:** Gives you a way to visualise, report and make data and insight available

- **Smart data services:** Data services that support the underlying operations, internal and external customers

Once you have this described, you can use it to better understand the maturity and priority in each of the capabilities. It also provides a way to understand dependencies between different parts of the ecosystem. You can even use the Level Up Framework to map where each capability is in terms of maturity – some capabilities are being established, some are advanced and can be accelerated at scale. It all helps to explain what your organisation needs and, more importantly, why.

More mature organisations that genuinely have data at the heart of the business are at the Accelerate or Optimise stage discussed in the book. In such organisations, you can imagine that data (or insight or analytics or equivalent) would be a capability in its own right on the main business capability map alongside product development, supply chain management and so on. This would be a very clear indication that data and AI are key capabilities for an organisation.

As this book has shown, data really does mean business, and business really does mean data. We hope we have shaped your thinking, given you tips for how to progress, sharpened your strategy and most of all, helped to level up your organisation to adapt, evolve and scale in an ever-changing world.

Enjoy the ride!

Acknowledgements

Having known each other for a number of years and in conversation over a drink at an industry event, we realised that we were both considering investing time and energy into writing a book. One was a book of 'recipes' to address issues that data and business professionals encounter – with ingredients, methods and utensils to help in those situations. The other – a 'no bullshit data strategy' book – was aimed at demystifying the world of data and delivering value using a no-nonsense business-focused approach.

A whiteboard session later, we realised we both had complementary thoughts, ideas, experiences and approaches that we've seen work across a broad range of industries and organisations. This session motivated us to put pen to paper, where the basis of this book was born, and over the following weeks and months, our thoughts and the story of what we wanted to say evolved into the first edition.

That was back in 2022. In the intervening years between the first and second editions being published, we continued to play the role of CDO, lead data strategy, and interact with, advise and deliver for CDOs and organisations across the globe, so we dusted off the pen and added some updates.

Aside from the support we have given each other through the process of putting this second edition together, we have a lifetime's worth of people we'd like to thank for helping us get here.

Jason Foster

Writing this book was a cathartic and amazing learning experience. It was the culmination of twenty-five years working in a vibrant, growing and thoroughly inspiring industry. From my first boss to the latest LinkedIn connection request, every individual I engaged with is just looking to do something good in the world, and every single experience through those interactions has given me the foundations needed to put this work together.

Writing the first edition, the perfect combination of desire, motivation, time, creativity and levels of coffee needed to write ebbed and flowed. Much of it was written during the lockdowns of 2020 while balancing running a business, home schooling the children, sharing workspace with the family and with the pressures of the situation ever present. Whilst writing the second edition didn't have a pandemic and lockdowns to manage around, the life pressures, in different guises, remained. So, I couldn't have finished this book without the help and support of so many people around me.

To my amazing wife, Victoria, for giving me time and space to think about and write this book. For listening to my updates and emotional state of mind about the writing process and giving me words of encouragement. To my children, Oliver and Alexander, for showing genuine interest and pride in the fact that Dad has written a book.

A special thanks to Jagpal Jheeta, who has been a boss, colleague, co-founder, industry peer, advisor and friend for the best part of twenty years. Without him my company, Cynozure, would never have happened and therefore it is unlikely this book would exist.

Finally, I would like to thank the whole Cynozure crew, new and old, for being such an epic and diverse team with a wonderful set of shared values and vision to help us and our customers succeed. You have all helped, directly or indirectly, this book – its cover, content, the methodologies and everything about it. We will grow, fail and succeed together. This one's for you.

Barry Green

The second time around the ideas were clear and the updates necessary: the change Gen AI has brought, the poor economic performance of the West and in society where a divisive approach seems to be the norm. This necessitates a way to think both pragmatically and use cogitative diversity as a weapon to create positive challenge and ideas.

For those who have allowed me to shape and create new ideas; thank you to the Bank of Ireland, Allianz Insurance and Premium Credit, who knew they needed to change and took a chance on my approach. A special thanks to Jeroen and the team at DSM (now dsm-firmenich) who helped facilitate a complete rethink of my approach at a strategic level.

I would also like to thank Andy at DSM who helped me prove that a lot can be done by a few people in sync. Also to Craig at CLR impact whose whole focus is data for good.

A special thanks to James Cobb who sponsored my Executive EMBA, and Peter Horton and Pauline Lockett for giving me a chance to develop personally. These two events changed my career and have allowed me to evolve.

Lastly, to my partner Violina, who is always a pillar I can rely on. And to my son Lochlan, whose childhood is infinitely more complex than mine. The idea of using AI and data to enhance our society is very personal, so our children don't continue to make the same mistakes of the past.

Together, we would like to also raise thanks to the data industry as a whole – a wonderful thriving community full of passionate and outstanding individuals, many of you trying, succeeding and evolving these methods in this book and learning together. We thank you all and hope this book does our industry justice and provides a reference material for years to come.

Of course, to the fantastic Rethink Press team who have once again smoothly and effortlessly helped take a book we wrote and turned it into a book that can be read. Special thanks to Eve and Anke for their guidance and making the process smooth and easy to engage with once again.

Finally, we wanted to thank those who have contributed to the book directly with their stories that have ended up quoted in the book. To Beatrice, Philip, Ellie, Jagpal, Susie, Ryan, Graeme, Pete, Anne-Claire, Neil, Victoria, Kim, Greg, Timo and Rob – thank you for trusting us with your comments and stories to sit alongside our material. These real-world lessons are so invaluable to support our experiences and to bring everything to life. For that we thank you.

The Authors

Jason Foster is a strategist working at the intersection of business, digital, data and AI. He has spent his career advising and working hands-on with organisations across the world on embedding data and AI into their business strategies. He cares deeply about creating a better future for all through the positive use of data and puts that at the heart of his work and his business.

In 2016, Jason set up Cynozure, a data and AI strategy company that helps organisations to better understand and activate their data to achieve business growth and better outcomes. Jason educates and presents to thousands of data, business and technology professionals each year. He actively works to promote data leadership through his global members club, the CDO Hub, which acts as a progressive and peer-to-peer learning accelerator for CDOs. He also hosts a podcast, *Hub & Spoken*, where he explores how organisations add value through the application of data and AI.

🌐 www.cynozure.com

in www.linkedin.com/in/jasonbfoster

 **Barry Green** is a future thinking Transformation leader who is passionate about using data for good and enabling digital to enhance the way we conduct business and our personal lives. His focus is on facilitating organisation change at all levels to achieve business objectives. He has a pragmatic execution style delivered with honest and robust challenge. He has undertaken a number of CDO roles with a strong belief that resilience, cognitive diversity and people are the keys to successful change and transformation, especially data. In his CDO roles, he has been building and testing his ideas on what it means to be a modern data/transformation leader. He has cross industry experience and recognises that while industries are different, there is a considerable amount that is the same. He has learned from his mistakes and

loves coming up with innovative ways to solve problems. He recognises that evolving ideas and building on existing foundations is key to success in an ever-changing world where pace and white noise create too many hype cycles.

in www.linkedin.com/in/barrycontinuium